The
Chicago High Schools
Report Card

SECOND EDITION

A Guide to Finding the Right
School for Your Child

Linda A. Thornton

CHICAGO
REVIEW
PRESS

Library of Congress Cataloging-in-Publication Data

Thornton, Linda A.
    The Chicago high schools report card : a guide to finding the right
school for your child / Linda A. Thornton. — 2nd ed.
        p. cm.
    Includes index.
    ISBN-13: 978-1-55652-611-4
    ISBN-10: 1-55652-611-3
        1. High schools—Illinois—Chicago—Directories.
        2. Education, Secondary—Illinois—Chicago—Directories.
    I. Title.
    L903.I35C58   2006
    373.025'77311
                                                            2005030076

Cover design: Rachel McClain
Cover photos: (top) Digital Vision/Getty Images; (bottom) Ryan McVay/
Getty Images
Interior design: Pamela Juárez

The author has made every effort to ensure that all the listing information is correct and current at the time of publication.

© 2006 by Linda A. Thornton
All rights reserved
Published by Chicago Review Press, Incorporated
814 North Franklin Street
Chicago, Illinois 60610
ISBN-10: 1-55652-611-3
ISBN-13: 978-1-55652-611-4
Printed in the United States of America
5 4 3 2 1

To Michael and Alexander:
the other two peas in my pod.

To my Mom and Dad:
my guiding lights.

Contents

Other High School Options

Acknowledgments

In writing this book, I've come to find out that it is not the solitary process I thought it would be. I would like to thank everyone that played a part in its development.

To Michael and Alexander for your wise counsel, your unwavering support and all those cups of tea. I couldn't have accomplished this without you two.

To my Mom, my Dad and my "Titi" Lucy for always making me feel so special and for passing on to me your sense of humor and your zest for life.

To all the Chicago educators I've had the privilege to meet for sharing your knowledge and supporting my book with such enthusiasm.

To Chicago Review Press for accepting my book for publication (one of the happiest days of my life!) and devoting so much time and attention to it. Special thanks to Cynthia Sherry, Associate Publisher; Brooke Kush, Project Editor; Allison Felus, Production Editor; Gerilee Hundt, Managing Editor; Michelle Niebur, Publicist; and Jon Hahn, Editorial Assistant.

Introduction

A Unique Admissions Process

With over one hundred high schools to choose from, Chicago families no longer assume that their students will be attending their local high school. The choices range from Catholic, independent, public, and a growing number of other options; the decisions continue from there. As a parent, will you pay tuition for your child to attend a private high school or will you send him or her to a free public high school? Will your child go to school close to home or face a long daily commute? And once you and your child have chosen a school, will that school accept your child? What are the admissions policies and protocol? Which school's philosophy is best suited to your child? How do you go about making this very important decision?

The entire process is stressful, competitive, and intimidating. I first began to hear parents talk of the high school quandary back when my son was in 4th grade. By the time he was in middle school, parents (myself included) were beginning to panic. Was it true that just because you lived near one of the public selective enrollment schools, you could not automatically attend? Did I hear that as many as 1,000 students are apt to take the Catholic placement exam at a given school that only has a freshman class of 350 students? Were some families actually forced to move from the city when their child was not accepted to any Chicago high school?

At that point, I decided to invest in a "how-to" book that would guide my family through the process. I was surprised to find that no such book existed; there was no single source of information. I began organizing my questions and the information I had already gathered into a spreadsheet for my own use. Friends began calling me to verify information or to share new findings. Then, through word of mouth, I began receiving phone calls from parents I didn't even know who were also desperate for timely and accurate information. It was then I realized how important it was for a book on this subject to exist.

The Research Process

I began by contacting the high school administrators at each of the school headquarters, principals at the grammar and high school levels, and parents in order to compile a list of high schools in and around the Chicago area (city and suburbs).

I developed a questionnaire and expanded on it after listening to the admission presentations at high school fairs, interviewing parents, and speaking with grammar school teachers and principals. It seemed important to be objective; personal opinions were not what families were looking for. Presenting the facts and suggesting a "plan of attack" would be more beneficial than critiquing each school, since this was a highly individualized process for each family.

I sent a mailing to each school requesting them to review and/or complete the questionnaire. Additional information was obtained from school visits, interviews at high school fairs and grammar school presentations, telephone interviews, school brochures, and Web sites. Each school reviewed its material and every effort was made to ensure that the information in this book was accurate at the time of publication.

How the Book Is Organized

Schools are divided into four categories: Catholic, public, independent, and other options (those not fitting into the first three categories); these are subclassified by gender (boys, girls, coed) and listed in alphabetical order. Public schools covered in this edition are within the Chicago city limits; Catholic, independent, and other options discussed are located in both the city and suburbs. Schools named after a person are listed alphabetically by that person's last name; those named after a saint are listed under "St." alphabetically by the saint's name. Please note that there are also three indexes: alphabetically by school name, by tuition classification, and by zip code of the school.

When I realized that I was not familiar with many of the terms used in the admissions process, I decided that parents would appreciate clear, concise explanations. Throughout the book you will find clarification of these terms. Refer to the Resource Guide for more helpful information.

Parents interviewed agreed that what to do and when to do it were the most confusing and intimidating aspects of the process. Likewise, grammar school administrators felt they were constantly reminding families of the time constraints. With this in mind, the "Steps for High School Admission" were developed.

The Book No Parent Should Be Without

The Chicago High Schools Report Card demystifies the complicated high school admissions process. It lists over one hundred schools by category and provides you with all the information you need to choose the right school for your child. Finally, it shares the best-kept secret of all: how to spread the search process over your child's middle school years, eliminate the stress, and enjoy an important family experience.

"Knowledge Is Power" —Sir Francis Bacon

Once you become aware that there are three to four times the number of students taking a placement exam at a given school than there are openings, it becomes apparent that there are more eager, qualified students than freshman openings at most Chicago area high schools. Therefore, securing the competitive edge becomes the all-important factor that will affect the next four years of your student's life and their ultimate success. Having all the information you require to make this very important decision will make your task much easier.

As I watch my high school–age son develop into a fine young man, I know that all of our family's research was worth it. He's made wonderful new friends, found a new school sport to join, and has become a member of an interesting school club, which has the added advantage of offering him some travel opportunities.

One morning, while getting dressed, I turned down the television volume and quickly got my husband's attention. We couldn't believe what we were hearing! Coming from my son's room at 7 A.M. was the sound of him whistling while getting ready for school. That's what I wish for you; a whistling high school student. The very best of luck to you.

Note to Readers

Parents gave a personal glimpse into their family's endeavor in the vignettes dispersed throughout the book. If you would like to share the experiences you had while searching for the right high school for your child, I would love to hear from you. Feel free to address mail to me: The Chicago High Schools Report Card, c/o Chicago Review Press, 814 N. Franklin Street, Chicago, IL 60610.

Steps for High School Admission

The Secret to a Stress-Free Experience

Many families begin the high school selection process during the fall of their child's 8th grade year. This gives a family only a couple of months to digest an abundance of information and make a decision, whether they have all their questions answered or not. Spreading out the search process over your child's middle school years, as outlined below, greatly lessens the stress factor and makes this very important family project an enjoyable experience.

Remember, the sooner your child gets excited over the prospect of high school and the more she hears just how important her middle school grades are (from someone other than you), the better equipped she will be to accomplish her goals.

6th Grade

I. Discuss School Choices

Parents should begin by discussing school choices without your child present. Have some ground rules set before you invite your child into the discussion. There is no point in selecting a school that is too far away, that is not in your budget, or just because your child's best friend is going there. There are several points to consider while discussing school choices:

School Type—Catholic, Independent, Public, or Other School Options Whether based around religious beliefs, a distinct educational philosophy, or a specific subject, each of these school types has a unique mission statement.

Coed vs. Single Gender According to research, there are gender differences in learning styles and some students do seem to excel in an all-boy or all-girl environment. For more information regarding gender-specific learning styles, see the Resource Guide.

Location of School and Daily Commute Decide how far is too far. Remember that your child will most likely be involved in extracurricular activities (sports, clubs, and organizations are an integral part of high school life) and will not be leaving school at dismissal time each day. Most high schools are accessible via public transportation, and discount Chicago Transit Authority (CTA) student passes are available for purchase. Call (888) 968-7282 or log on to www.transitchicago.com for travel information to a specific school.

School Size Where will your child fit best: the Chicago Waldorf School, with a recent freshman class of eighteen; Lane Tech High School, the largest high school in Illinois, with a recent freshman class of 1,100; or somewhere in between?

Evaluate the school's student to faculty ratio. This statistic compares the number of students to the number of teachers. Generally, the fewer students per teacher, the better the learning conditions.

School Costs   What is your high school budget? The highest tuition listed in this book is currently $20,000 per year; public schools are free.

Tuitions are constantly increasing. Their exact dollar amounts were not included in this book since they would soon be outdated. Instead, tuition amounts have been divided into five classifications (see the index by tuition classification). The amounts below are per school year and the percentage of schools that fall into that tuition classification is shown in parentheses:

$: Less than $6,000 (11%)
$$: $6,000–$8,000 (51%)
$$$: $8,000–$10,000 (14%)
$$$$: $10,000–$15,000 (5%)
$$$$$: Over $15,000 (19%)

In addition to tuition, other expenses include application and registration fees, books (book costs can total hundreds of dollars), uniforms, cafeteria meals, field trips, and club and social events. Also, be sure to ask about any fundraising and/or pledge obligations. In the school listings, under the school information heading titled "Other Expenditures," a "yes" indicates that, at the least, you can expect to encounter the costs discussed above; anything additional is indicated.

Consider financial aid; it is based solely on financial need and is not considered a loan. All applications are confidential and parents are encouraged not to be intimidated. A separate application along with a recent 1040 federal tax form is required and in most cases it is reviewed by an outside agency. Some schools may require that the student provide either work-study or fundraising volunteer hours.

Some high schools and community groups give scholarships based on a student's academic record and/or placement test score. This money goes toward tuition and is not considered a loan. It may be provided only one time or on a yearly basis as long as the student maintains a certain grade point average. See the individual school listings and the Resource Guide for more information about specific scholarships.

School Style and Your Child's Personality You know your child better than anyone; consider who he is and where he belongs: In a boarding school, a military academy, a progressive environment, or a traditional atmosphere? In a religion-based or a nondenominational institution? In a strict or a laid-back setting? Wearing a uniform or jeans each day?

Would your child benefit from block scheduling? This is a time restructuring of the school day, dividing it into four, eighty-one minute instructional blocks. It is believed that fewer daily classes allow for greater subject focus.

Student's Scholastic Ability You want the right academic setting so your child will thrive at his or her own level. Is your child an independent thinker or does she require constant monitoring? Will he become bored if he is not constantly challenged or is it enough of a challenge for him to do only what is required?

Most schools offer either a career or a college preparatory (prep) program. A career prep program prepares the student for a vocational field and may include college prep classes. A college prep program is a four-year course of study in preparation for college that includes English, social studies, science, math, world language, fine arts, physical education, and electives adding up to a total between 24 and 28 credits.

For the student who thrives on a demanding course load, success in these courses will add to his or her grade point average. An Honors course is a step up in difficulty and complexity from a college prep course. An Advanced Placement (AP) course is a challenging college-level academic course.

The International Baccalaureate (IB) Program was established in Switzerland in the 1960s as a demanding liberal arts curriculum and testing program that exposes students to the humanities and sciences. Graduation leads to an IB diploma, which is highly respected by top colleges and universities worldwide. Member schools move through three levels of classification as they complete the application process: prospective, affiliated, and finally, participating.

Talented and motivated 7th and 8th grade students with limited incomes can look into the many academic support and scholarship programs available (see the Resource Guide).

Some high schools have the added resources that allow them to offer additional assistance to students with diagnosed learning needs in the form of appropriately designed classes and programs.

2. Send for Brochures and View Web Sites

While a school's Web site will give you the factual information you are looking for, a brochure will romanticize the school. Have the brochures addressed to your child; it will make him feel important and keep him excited about his prospects.

3. Speak with Current High School Students and Their Families

What better way to get a firsthand view of the daily commutes, the school's personality, and both a parent's and student's point of view?

7th Grade

1. Time for Students to Start Preparing

Become familiar with the admission criteria. In addition to placement and/or entrance exams, high schools also place importance on middle school transcripts (especially 7th grade and the first semester of 8th grade), homework (completed on time), behavior (respect for authority and peers), and attendance (absences and tardiness). Schools have been known to reject students because of their tardiness record.

Become aware of any admission priority given and make sure to stress the fact that your child is within this group, whether it's religious, sibling, or legacy based.

Have your child begin preparing his student resume. At some point in the admissions process, she will be asked to list sports, social, and service activities in which she is involved in her school, church, and community. It is a good idea for your child to keep track of these activities and accomplishments for easy reference.

2. Attend High School Fairs

High school fairs are either sponsored by your child's grammar school or by a group of high schools. Each school is given an area in which to display brochures, photographs, and/or video presentations. In this informal setting, you have the opportunity to meet current students as well as the admissions directors, who are on hand to "sell" their school and to answer your questions. These fairs offer a practical way to obtain an overview of a variety of schools and may entice you to visit a school or, if you have already visited, help you obtain the answers to those questions you did not ask on your first visit.

3. Attend High School Open Houses

Most schools set aside certain days when families are invited to visit for a full tour of the facility and the opportunity to meet students and faculty. Contact the individual school for its schedule.

4. Obtain Input from Your Child's Current Grammar School

Schedule a meeting with your child's current teachers and principal. They interact with your child every day; find out what their top school choices would be for your child and why.

If you need their assistance, ask for it. During the selection process, it is not unusual for a grade school to interact with a high school on a student's behalf by writing a letter of recommendation and/or attempting to convince the high school to accept a student they have turned down. Likewise, high schools will keep grade schools abreast of their former students' success.

5. Begin Narrowing Down Your Choices

Take some time to review your selections. Do you and your child agree on which schools would be best? Is more discussion required?

8th Grade

I. Make Your Final High School Selections

It's time for the family to sit down and agree on the four or five schools that are a good fit.

2. Reattend the Open Houses of Your Top Choices

Concentrate on things you may have missed the first time around: Are the bathrooms graffiti free? What's featured in the display cases? How does the cafeteria look? Ask the students some questions: What do they like most and least about the school? How they did they come to choose this particular school? Was this their first choice school? What other schools did they apply to?

This is also a good time to review the school's application process. Make sure you pick up any forms you may need and pay particular attention to any deadline dates.

3. Students Should Sign Up for a Shadow Day at Top Choices

Most high schools offer prospective students the opportunity to attend a typical day of classes with a current student (most often, a recent graduate of their grammar school whom they know) and be their "shadow" for the day to get a feel for the school. Contact the individual school to see if there are specific shadow days planned or whether an appointment is necessary.

4. Parents Should Visit Top Choices on Their Own on a Regular School Day

Just a 10-minute walk down the hall as classes change can give you much information.

Do you hear abusive language from the students? Are students moving briskly to their next class? Are teachers herding students or civilly conversing with them?

5. Begin the Application Process

Have your child complete the applications, and be sure to keep copies for yourself. If a placement exam is involved, ask each school what test they will be using, as these may change from year to year. If your child is planning to take the Catholic high school placement exam, remember not to schedule any other exams on that date as many Catholic high schools test on the same day.

Follow up with your child's current school to make sure that the high schools you are applying to have received the information they have requested (transcripts, records, etc.) by their deadline dates. School records including disciplinary issues, attendance, and tardiness are also shared. A parent or guardian must sign a release form before the school will release any information.

6. Students Should Prepare for Placement Exams

Educators interviewed strongly believed that students who are familiar and comfortable with the exam format will have the advantage when taking it. Exam review books—available at area bookstores and libraries—give students a brief description of the exam, skill review, and some practice exams with answers and explanations. Educators also noted the importance of taking the time to read directions thoroughly and reading every answer before making a choice.

7. Students Should Take the Placement Exams

Depending on your choice of Catholic, independent, public, or other school options, your child could be taking up to four exams, so make sure to plan accordingly when scheduling exam dates. Remember that the Catholic school placement exam should be taken at your first choice school; some Catholic schools will only accept test scores from their school.

Find out ahead of time what needs to be brought to the test: pens, pencils, a calculator, and/or the exam fee. Lay it all out the night before. Make sure your child gets a good night's sleep and arrives early at the exam site; you will be surprised at the number of students there (at times, the Chicago police have been called in to ease traffic flow around a school). The exams are long and it's a good idea to bring a water bottle and a granola bar.

8. Finally, the Results Come In

If your child was accepted to his or her first choice, congratulations! Notify your grammar school of the good news. In the case of Catholic schools, if your child was rejected, ask if they can send her test scores on to her second choice school. If she was placed on a wait list, remember that during the next couple of weeks students who have tested at more than one school will be making their final choice, which will move her up the ladder.

Catholic High Schools

Introduction

The Archdiocese of Chicago is the largest nonpublic school system in the world. Sponsored either by a particular religious order or by the Archdiocese of Chicago, Catholic high schools offer a faith-based education in which the Catholic doctrine is an integral part of the curriculum. They also offer the opportunity for a single-gender education. Nearly half of the schools in the archdiocese are either boys' or girls' schools. According to research, there are gender differences in learning styles. For more information regarding gender-specific learning styles, see the Resource Guide.

Each year, on the second Saturday in January, a three and a half hour placement exam is given at each of the Catholic high schools. One of the three basic tests (Terranova, STS Placement, or ACT) is given; their scores are interchangeable. It is very important that students test at their first choice school since some high schools will not accept test scores from another school. Admission decisions are mailed in mid-February.

When you are reviewing Catholic school options, look for special designations and awards given to schools. Only 2% of U.S. schools are named Blue Ribbon Schools, a distinction given by a national program honoring public and private grammar and secondary schools for either their academic superiority or their substantial gains in student achievement (see www.ed.gov, search: blue ribbon schools). *U.S. News & World Report* included many of the area's Catholic high schools in their report of outstanding high schools.

Since every school offers financial aid, no separate heading for it appears in the individual school listings. There are literally millions of dollars made available each year to those students who qualify.

Some Catholic grammar schools plan a Catholic high school fair for their interested families. This is a great way to obtain an overview of many schools, which may entice you to plan a visit or to give a school a second look. For timely information on Catholic high school fairs, call the Archdiocese Office of Catholic Schools at (312) 751-5200.

Catholic High Schools: Boys

Catholic High Schools: Girls

Catholic High Schools: Coed

Archbishop Quigley Preparatory Seminary High School

103 East Chestnut Street Chicago, IL 60611
Phone Number: (312) 787-9343
Fax Number: (312) 787-9167

Web Site: www.quigley.org
E-mail: info@quigley.org
Principal: Rev. Peter Snieg
Admissions Contact: Mr. Brian Condon
Gender: Boys

Total Enrollment: 220   *Student to Faculty Ratio:* 7:1
Number of Freshmen: 60   *Percentage of College Bound Grads:* 98%
Average Class Size: 15–20   *Tuition:* $$

Other Expenditures: Yes, also fundraising
Academic Specialty: College prep
Honors/Advanced Placement Classes: Yes
International Baccalaureate Program: No
Resources, Special Learning Needs: No
Profile: Est. 1905. Gold Coast. Historic 1917 Gothic-style building. Students are asked to consider the priesthood. Solid athletic program. Listed in *U.S. News & World Report*'s "96 Outstanding American High Schools," January 1999.
Unique Traits: Seminary status, location
Public Transportation:
      CTA L: Red Line Chicago
      CTA Bus: Michigan
Dress Code: Dress slacks, shirt, and tie—3 days; polo shirt or shirt with collar—2 days
Admission Requirements: Baptized and confirmed Roman Catholic, application, placement exam, pastor and principal recommendations
Academic Scholarships: Full, half, and quarter

Brother Rice High School

10001 South Pulaski Road Chicago, IL 60655
Phone Number: (773) 429-4300
Fax Number: (773) 779-5239

Web Site: www.brrice.org
E-mail: tlyons@brrice.org
Principal: Mr. James P. Antos
Admissions Contact: Mr. Tim Lyons
Gender: Boys

Total Enrollment: 1,200   *Student to Faculty Ratio:* 15:1
Number of Freshmen: 350   *Percentage of College Bound Grads:* 94%
Average Class Size: 20–35   *Tuition:* $$

Other Expenditures: Yes, also fundraising
Academic Specialty: College prep
Honors/Advanced Placement Classes: Yes
International Baccalaureate Program: No
Resources, Special Learning Needs: Yes
Profile: Est. 1956. Mt. Greenwood. Curriculum based on the philosophy
of Br. Edmund Ignatius Rice, founder of the Congregation of Christian Brothers. Twice named "One of the Top Fifty Outstanding High Schools in the Nation" by the Catholic High School Honor Roll.
Unique Traits: Largest private boys high school in the nation, located next to Mother McAuley High School, the largest private girls high school in the nation.
Public Transportation:
    CTA Bus: Pulaski
Dress Code: Solid color slacks, solid color button-down shirt and tie or polo shirt, dress shoes
Admission Requirements: Placement exam
Academic Scholarships: Yes, based on placement exam

Hales Franciscan High School

4930 South Cottage Grove Avenue Chicago, IL 60615
Phone Number: (773) 285-8400
Fax Number: (773) 285-7025

Web Site: www.halesfranciscan.org
E-mail: jaystrong@yahoo.com
Principal: Mr. John L. Young
Admissions Contact: Mr. Jasper Strong
Gender: Boys

Total Enrollment: 260   *Student to Faculty Ratio:* 13:1
Number of Freshmen: 89   *Percentage of College Bound Grads:* 100%
Average Class Size: 17   *Tuition:* $

Other Expenditures: Yes
Academic Specialty: College prep
Honors/Advanced Placement Classes: Yes
International Baccalaureate Program: No
Resources, Special Learning Needs: No
Profile: Est. 1962. Hyde Park. Predominantly African American student
   population. Small size allows for academic development, aware-
   ness, and respect of cultural heritage. Recognized as a Blue Ribbon
   School.
Unique Traits: One of three Catholic high schools in the country dedicated
   to African American males
Public Transportation:
      CTA Bus: Cottage Grove
Dress Code: Khaki slacks, white button-down shirt, tie, dress shoes
Admission Requirements: Placement exam, transcripts
Academic Scholarships: 100%, 50% based on placement exam percentile

Leo High School

7901 South Sangamon Street Chicago, IL 60620
Phone Number: (773) 224-9600
Fax Number: (773) 224-3856

Web Site: www.leohighschool.org
E-mail: administration@leohighschool.org
Principal: Mr. Robert M. Kman
Admissions Contact: Mr. Noah Cannon
Gender: Boys

Total Enrollment: 310   *Student to Faculty Ratio:* 20:1
Number of Freshmen: 85   *Percentage of College Bound Grads:* 90%
Average Class Size: 25   *Tuition:* $

Other Expenditures: Yes
Academic Specialty: College prep
Honors/Advanced Placement Classes: Yes
International Baccalaureate Program: No
Resources, Special Learning Needs: Yes
Profile: Est. 1926. Gresham. Urban minority student population. The only
    school in Illinois to offer Learning Logic computer-based programs
    developed by the National Science Foundation.
Unique Traits: Specialized computer programs
Public Transportation:
    CTA Bus: Halsted
Dress Code: Dark slacks, white shirt, black tie, no sneakers
Admission Requirements: Placement exam
Academic Scholarships: No

Mount Carmel High School

6410 South Dante Avenue Chicago, IL 60637
Phone Number: (773) 324-1020
Fax Number: (773) 324-9235

Web Site: www.mchs.org
E-mail: bnolan@mchs.org
Principal: Fr. Carl Markelz, O.Carm
Admissions Contact: Mr. William Nolan
Gender: Boys

Total Enrollment: 780   *Student to Faculty Ratio:* 24:1
Number of Freshmen: 210   *Percentage of College Bound Grads:* 95%
Average Class Size: 23–25   *Tuition:* $$

Other Expenditures: Yes, also fundraising
Academic Specialty: College prep
Honors/Advanced Placement Classes: Yes
International Baccalaureate Program: No
Resources, Special Learning Needs: Yes
Profile: Est. 1900. Woodlawn. More state sports championships than any other high school in the archdiocese. First private Chicago high school to be honored by the U.S. Department of Education as an exemplary private school.
Unique Traits: Championship sports program
Public Transportation:
　　Metra: 63rd
　　Bus: Mount Carmel bus available at an extra cost (call school for routes)
Dress Code: Dress slacks, school polo shirt, no sneakers
Admission Requirements: Placement exam
Academic Scholarships: $1,000, $2,000, full tuition based on placement exam (freshman year only)

Notre Dame High School

7655 West Dempster Street Niles, IL 60714
Phone Number: (847) 965-2900
Fax Number: (847) 965-2975

Web Site: www.ndhsdons.org
E-mail: lbontempo@ndhsdons.org
Principal: Mr. Steven Zeier
Admissions Contact: Mr. Dennis Zelasko
Gender: Boys

Total Enrollment: 780   *Student to Faculty Ratio:* 17:1
Number of Freshmen: 210   *Percentage of College Bound Grads:* 97%
Average Class Size: 25   *Tuition:* $$

Other Expenditures: Yes, also activities fee
Academic Specialty: College prep
Honors/Advanced Placement Classes: Yes
International Baccalaureate Program: No
Resources, Special Learning Needs: Yes
Profile: Est. 1955. Based on the educational tradition of the Congregation
of the Holy Cross (faith, scholarship, and service), whose priests are
still an active part of the teaching staff today.
Unique Traits: Medium-sized school with a 28-acre campus
Public Transportation:
     Pace Bus: Dempster
Dress Code: Khaki or dress slacks, polo shirt
Admission Requirements: Placement exam
Academic Scholarships: $1,000 based on placement exam

St. Lawrence Seminary High School

301 Church Street Mt. Calvary, WI 53057
Phone Number: (920) 753-7500
Fax Number: (920) 753-7507

Web Site: www.stlawrence.edu
E-mail: jjakobek@stlawrence.edu
Principal: Fr. Dennis Druggan
Admissions Contact: Ms. Jennifer Jakobek
Gender: Boys

Total Enrollment: 220   *Student to Faculty Ratio:* 10:1

Number of Freshmen: 65   *Percentage of College Bound Grads:* 98%

Average Class Size: 17   *Tuition:* $$ includes room, board, books, and fees

Other Expenditures: No

Academic Specialty: College prep

Honors/Advanced Placement Classes: No

International Baccalaureate Program: No

Resources, Special Learning Needs: No

Profile: Est. 1860. Boarding school. 13 buildings on 80 acres. Owned and operated by the Capuchin-Franciscan Friars. Diverse student population (United States and abroad).

Unique Traits: Boarding school, multicultural

Public Transportation: N/A

Dress Code: Khaki slacks, shirt with collar, shirt and tie on Sundays

Admission Requirements: Must be Catholic, in the 50+ percentile of the placement exam

Academic Scholarships: N/A

St. Patrick High School

5900 West Belmont Avenue Chicago, IL 60634
Phone Number: (773) 282-8844
Fax Number: (773) 282-3538

Web Site: www.stpatrick.org
E-mail: dgalante@stpatrick.org
Principal: Dr. Joseph Schmidt
Admissions Contact: Mr. Dan Galante
Gender: Boys

Total Enrollment: 1,013   *Student to Faculty Ratio:* 20:1
Number of Freshmen: 287   *Percentage of College Bound Grads:* 95%
Average Class Size: 28   *Tuition:* $$

Other Expenditures: Yes
Academic Specialty: College prep
Honors/Advanced Placement Classes: Yes
International Baccalaureate Program: No
Resources, Special Learning Needs: Yes
Profile: Est. 1861. Northwest side. Founded by the Christian Brothers. Chicago's oldest and one of the largest Catholic boys high schools. Major million-dollar renovation in 2001.
Unique Traits: Above-average student to computer ratio
Public Transportation:
    CTA Bus: Belmont
    Bus: St. Patrick bus available at an extra cost (call school for routes)
Dress Code: Dress slacks, shirt with collar, no sneakers
Admission Requirements: Placement exam
Academic Scholarships: Based on placement exam

St. Rita of Cascia High School

7740 South Western Avenue Chicago, IL 60620
Phone Number: (773) 925-6600
Fax Number: (773) 925-6582

Web Site: www.stritahs.com
E-mail: jquinn@stritahs.com
Principal: Fr. Tom McCarthy
Admissions Contact: Mr. John Quinn
Gender: Boys

Total Enrollment: 800   *Student to Faculty Ratio:* 18:1
Number of Freshmen: 220   *Percentage of College Bound Grads:* 97%
Average Class Size: 18   *Tuition:* $$

Other Expenditures: Yes
Academic Specialty: College prep
Honors/Advanced Placement Classes: Yes
International Baccalaureate Program: No
Resources, Special Learning Needs: Yes
Profile: Est. 1905. Wrightwood. In the Augustinian tradition of truth, unity, and love. Recognized as a Blue Ribbon School and an Exemplary School by the U.S. Department of Education. Listed in *U.S. News & World Report*'s "96 Outstanding American High Schools," January 1999.
Unique Traits: 33-acre campus
Public Transportation:
          CTA Bus: Western
Dress Code: Dress slacks, polo shirt
Admission Requirements: Placement exam
Academic Scholarships: $2,000–$5,000 based on placement exam

A Winning Combination

A Catholic Boys High School Experience

By J.Q.

From the time my son was born, he's been one of those high-energy kids who would rather be outside perfecting his sports skills than inside studying. We've been involved with so many traveling teams that my friends tease me by saying our family must know every boy my son's age in the Chicago area.

When it came time to start thinking about high schools, I was frantic. Where would my son fit best? If the sports programs enticed him, would he pay attention to the academics? My son, however, had the same confidence and nonchalance about the decision as when he was sinking a winning basket or kicking a game-tying goal. But my husband surprised us both with his announcement: "What's all the fuss about?" In his mind, the school had already been chosen.

My husband had always been passionate about his alma mater, a Catholic boys school. He frequently told stories about how the brothers had helped him develop into the person he was today and how the many friendships that had begun in his youth had lasted over the years. However, I was stunned. It never occurred to me that the legacy would continue. The school seemed too far away, and I wasn't sure of its academic credentials. Meanwhile, my son was in a panic. While all his friends were applying to the same schools, he was convinced he'd be attending this one all alone—without a girl in sight.

My husband had spent previous years recruiting for his alma mater, and now put all of his energy into recruiting students from our son's grammar school. He even planned an informational session based around a basketball scrimmage in the high school's gym to entice the boys to visit. After the game, students and parents were taken on an informal tour of the school, which was followed with a question and answer period and pizza dinner.

It was at one of these sessions that I learned that while this school enjoyed an overwhelming amount of state sports championships, it also had received impressive accolades from the educational community. The distance to the school seemed less daunting as I heard the teachers discuss the organized car pools that ferried students all around the city. I was surprised to discover that geographic boundaries are not as rigid as they used to be (South Siders now actually venture north and North Siders will travel south), partly due to better transportation—sometimes there is better public transportation to a school that is farther away. In this case, taking the L and then jumping on a Metra train was a very attractive option. And then when I overheard some students telling my son about the interaction between their school and other Catholic girls schools, I started to realize that this very well could be the best place for my son for the next four years.

That year, my son and two other students from his grammar school class applied and were accepted to this high school. He has made every team he's tried out for, and my husband and I still attend every sporting event there, whether our son is on the team or not. The personal attention he's received has made a big difference in his academic performance. He'd still rather be kicking, throwing, or shooting a ball, but now he's also able to focus and use the study skills he's gained in order to be successful.

Josephinum Academy

1501 North Oakley Boulevard Chicago, IL 60622
Phone Number: (773) 276-1261
Fax Number: (773) 292-3963

Web Site: www.josephinum.org
E-mail: See website
Principal: Sr. Martha Roughan
Admissions Contact: Ms. Courtney Phillips
Gender: Girls

Total Enrollment: 180	*Student to Faculty Ratio:* 5:1
Number of Freshmen: 45	*Percentage of College Bound Grads:* 80%
Average Class Size: 12	*Tuition:* $

Other Expenditures: Yes
Academic Specialty: College prep
Honors/Advanced Placement Classes: Yes
International Baccalaureate Program: No
Resources, Special Learning Needs: No
Profile: Est. 1890. Wicker Park. Affordable inner-city high school providing faith-built education to multicultural young women.
Unique Traits: Small class size and personalized attention
Public Transportation:
   CTA L: Blue Line Damen
   CTA Bus: North, Western
Dress Code: Blue slacks or skirt, white school polo shirt
Admission Requirements: Placement exam, transcripts, discipline, attendance, essay
Academic Scholarships: N/A

Maria High School

6727 South California Avenue Chicago, IL 60629
Phone Number: (773) 925-8686
Fax Number: (773) 925-8885

Web Site: www.mariahighschool.org
E-mail: bwhitehouse@mariahighschool.org
Principal: Sr. Nancy Gannon, SFCC
Admissions Contact: Miss Bridget Whitehouse
Gender: Girls

Total Enrollment: 500   *Student to Faculty Ratio:* 14:1
Number of Freshmen: 125   *Percentage of College Bound Grads:* 98%
Average Class Size: 20   *Tuition:* $$

Other Expenditures: No—all inclusive; no book fees or fundraising requirements
Academic Specialty: College prep
Honors/Advanced Placement Classes: Yes
International Baccalaureate Program: No
Resources, Special Learning Needs: Yes
Profile: Est. 1952. Marquette Park. Flexible curriculum to meet the needs of different academic levels. Awarded the 2002 National Service Learning Leader School Award, a service learning grant from the Chicago Community Trust.
Unique Traits: Medium-sized school with large school opportunities
Public Transportation:
     CTA L: Orange Line Western
     CTA Bus: California private bus transportation available at an extra cost (call school for routes)
Dress Code: Gray slacks or skirt, each class wears different school polo shirt
Admission Requirements: Placement exam, transcripts
Academic Scholarships: $500 and $1,000 each year, based on placement exam

Mother McAuley Liberal Arts High School

3737 West 99th Street Chicago, IL 60655
Phone Number: (773) 881-6500
Fax Number: (773) 881-6562

Web Site: www.mothermcauley.org
E-mail: cwhite@mothermcauley.org
Principal: Sr. Rose Wiorek, RSM
Admissions Contact: Ms. Colleen White
Gender: Girls

Total Enrollment: 1,650   *Student to Faculty Ratio:* 16:1
Number of Freshmen: 410   *Percentage of College Bound Grads:* 99%
Average Class Size: 26   *Tuition:* $$

Other Expenditures: Yes
Academic Specialty: College prep
Honors/Advanced Placement Classes: Yes
International Baccalaureate Program: No
Resources, Special Learning Needs: Yes
Profile: Est. 1846. Southwest side. Nationally recognized, faith-based educational programs. Largest Catholic girls high school in the U.S. Recognized as a Blue Ribbon School.
Unique Traits: Premier state-of-the-art fine arts program and facilities
Public Transportation:
    CTA Bus: Pulaski
Dress Code: Skirt, school polo shirt (each class level votes)
Admission Requirements: Placement exam
Academic Scholarships: 50% of tuition, $1,000 leadership award based on placement exam, $500 for students of alumnae

Mount Assisi Academy

13860 Main Street Lemont, IL 60439
Phone Number: (630) 257-7844
Fax Number: (630) 257-6362

Web Site: www.mtassisiacademy.org
E-mail: admissions@mtassisiacademy.org
Principal: Sr. Mary Francis Werner, OSF
Admissions Contact: Ms. Lori Tondini
Gender: Girls

Total Enrollment: 310   *Student to Faculty Ratio:* 20:1
Number of Freshmen: 80   *Percentage of College Bound Grads:* 98%
Average Class Size: 15–20 *Tuition:* $

Other Expenditures: Yes
Academic Specialty: College prep
Honors/Advanced Placement Classes: Yes
International Baccalaureate Program: No
Resources, Special Learning Needs: Yes
Profile: Est. 1951. Franciscan ideals. Nurturing the student's intellectual, spiritual, physical, emotional, cultural, and technological growth.
Unique Traits: Small community setting
Public Transportation: N/A
Dress Code: Each year wears different color plaid skirt, white blouse, school sweater
Admission Requirements: Transcripts
Academic Scholarships: Two available (freshmen)

Notre Dame High School

3000 North Mango Avenue Chicago, IL 60634
Phone Number: (773) 622-9494
Fax Number: (773) 622-8511

Web Site: www.ndhs4girls.org
E-mail: kbooth@ndhs4girls.org
Principal: Ms. Staci Viola
Admissions Contact: Ms. Karen Booth
Gender: Girls

Total Enrollment: 350   *Student to Faculty Ratio:* 18:1
Number of Freshmen: 105   *Percentage of College Bound Grads:* 95%
Average Class Size: 20   *Tuition:* $$

Other Expenditures: Yes
Academic Specialty: College prep
Honors/Advanced Placement Classes: Yes
International Baccalaureate Program: No
Resources, Special Learning Needs: Yes
Profile: Est. 1938. Northwest side. Rich, multicultural environment.
   Vibrant spiritual community. Recognized as a Blue Ribbon School.
Unique Traits: Entrepreneurial leadership programs
Public Transportation:
   CTA Bus: Central, Diversey, Austin, Belmont
Dress Code: Skirt, polo shirt, sweater
Admission Requirements: Placement exam
Academic Scholarships: Up to $5,000 based on placement exam

Our Lady of Tepeyac High School

2228 South Whipple Street Chicago, IL 60623
Phone Number: (773) 522-0023
Fax Number: (773) 522-0508

Web Site: www.tepeyachighschool.org
E-mail: kingram@aol.com
Principal: Ms. Joni Thompson
Admissions Contact: Ms. Isabel Del Real
Gender: Girls

Total Enrollment: 185	*Student to Faculty Ratio:* 25:1
Number of Freshmen: 65	*Percentage of College Bound Grads:* 90%
Average Class Size: 25	*Tuition:* $

Other Expenditures: Yes
Academic Specialty: College prep
Honors/Advanced Placement Classes: Yes
International Baccalaureate Program: No
Resources, Special Learning Needs: Yes
Profile: Est. 1928. Pilsen/Little Village. Serving mostly Latin and African American students. Dedicated to strengthening faith and academics through community.
Unique Traits: The only Catholic girls high school in Pilsen/Little Village area
Public Transportation:
    CTA L: Blue Line California, Kedzie
    CTA Bus: 26th
Dress Code: Skirt (each class wears different color), white blouse with collar
Admission Requirements: Placement exam
Academic Scholarships: Based on placement exam

Queen of Peace High School

7659 South Linder Avenue Burbank, IL 60459
Phone Number: (708) 458-7600
Fax Number: (708) 458-5734

Web Site: www.queenofpeacehs.org
E-mail: See Web site
Principal: Ms. Patty Nolan-Fitzgerald
Admissions Contact: Ms. Elaine Whitehouse
Gender: Girls

Total Enrollment: 825   *Student to Faculty Ratio:* 15:1
Number of Freshmen: 205   *Percentage of College Bound Grads:* 100%
Average Class Size: 20   *Tuition:* $$

Other Expenditures: Yes
Academic Specialty: College prep
Honors/Advanced Placement Classes: Yes
International Baccalaureate Program: No
Resources, Special Learning Needs: No
Profile: Est. 1926. A Catholic Sinsinawa Dominican high school educating
    a diverse female population. Championship sports program.
Unique Traits: An empowering all-girls environment
Public Transportation:
    CTA *Bus:* 79th
    Pace *Bus:* 79th, Central
Dress Code: Uniform skirt and school sweater
Admission Requirements: Placement exam, transcripts
Academic Scholarships: Based on placement exam

Regina Dominican High School

701 Locust Road Wilmette, IL 60091
Phone Number: (847) 256-7660
Fax Number: (847) 256-3726

Web Site: www.rdhs.org
E-mail: pfuentes@rdhs.org
Principal: Ms. Kathy Rzany
Admissions Contact: Ms. Patricia Fuentes
Gender: Girls

Total Enrollment: 425	*Student to Faculty Ratio:* 12:1
Number of Freshmen: 122	*Percentage of College Bound Grads:* 100%
Average Class Size: 17	*Tuition:* $$$

Other Expenditures: Yes, also labs
Academic Specialty: College prep
Honors/Advanced Placement Classes: Yes
International Baccalaureate Program: No
Resources, Special Learning Needs: No
Profile: Est. 1958. Dedicated to academic excellence and Christian values. Students from multicultural and religious backgrounds. Enrollment is 50% city and 50% suburban.
Unique Traits: Small size fosters individual attention
Public Transportation:
> *Pace Bus:* Lake

Dress Code: Black or khaki slacks, plaid skirt (girls vote), assorted color school polo shirt
Admission Requirements: Placement exam
Academic Scholarships: Based on placement exam

Resurrection High School

7500 West Talcott Avenue Chicago, IL 60631
Phone Number: (773) 775-6616
Fax Number: (773) 775-0611

Web Site: www.reshs.org
E-mail: website@reshs.org
Principal: Ms. Jo Marie Yonkus
Admissions Contact: Ms. Laura Tully
Gender: Girls

Total Enrollment: 900   *Student to Faculty Ratio:* 13:1
Number of Freshmen: 220   *Percentage of College Bound Grads:* 95%
Average Class Size: 12   *Tuition:* $$

Other Expenditures: Yes
Academic Specialty: College prep
Honors/Advanced Placement Classes: Yes
International Baccalaureate Program: No
Resources, Special Learning Needs: Yes
Profile: Est. 1922. Northwest side. Listed in *U.S. News & World Report*'s "96 Outstanding High Schools," January 1999. Received 2002 Presidential Award; named a National Service Learning Leader School for its students' nonmandatory 41,000 community service hours.
Unique Traits: Practicum program provides credits and practical experience with mentors in various professional careers
Public Transportation:
   CTA L: Blue Line Harlem
   CTA Bus: Higgins
   Metra: Norwood Park
   Bus: Resurrection bus available at an extra cost (call for routes)
Dress Code: Slacks or skort, school polo shirt or sweater
Admission Requirements: Placement exam
Academic Scholarships: $500; $1,000 based on placement exam

St. Scholastica Academy

7416 North Ridge Boulevard Chicago, IL 60645
Phone Number: (773) 764-5715
Fax Number: (773) 764-0304

Web Site: www.scholastica.us
E-mail: jfurgason@scholastica.us
Principal: Ms. Anne Matz '85
Admissions Contact: Ms. Jamie Furgason
Gender: Girls

Total Enrollment: 300   *Student to Faculty Ratio:* 12:1
Number of Freshmen: 62   *Percentage of College Bound Grads:* 100%
Average Class Size: 15   *Tuition:* $$

Other Expenditures: Yes
Academic Specialty: College prep
Honors/Advanced Placement Classes: No
International Baccalaureate Program: Yes
Resources, Special Learning Needs: Yes (on an individual basis)
Profile: Est. 1865 (1906 at new location). Rogers Park. 14-acre campus. In
the tradition of Benedictine values; excellence in a supporting, respect-
ful, caring environment.
Unique Traits: Excellent value, affordable education
Public Transportation:
     CTA L: Red Line Howard
Dress Code: Khaki slacks or plaid skirt, polo shirt, sweater
Admission Requirements: Placement exam
Academic Scholarships: Up to 50% of tuition based on placement exam

Trinity High School

7574 West Division Street River Forest, IL 60305
Phone Number: (708) 771-8383
Fax Number: (708) 488-2014

Web Site: www.trinityhs.org
E-mail: ia@trinityhs.org
Principal: Ms. Michele Whitehead
Admissions Contact: Ms. Jessica Roche
Gender: Girls

Total Enrollment: 500   *Student to Faculty Ratio:* 13:1
Number of Freshmen: 135   *Percentage of College Bound Grads:* 100%
Average Class Size: 20   *Tuition:* $$

Other Expenditures: Yes
Academic Specialty: College prep
Honors/Advanced Placement Classes: Yes
International Baccalaureate Program: Yes
Resources, Special Learning Needs: No
Profile: Est. 1918. In the Dominican tradition of spiritual, intellectual, social, and moral development. First Catholic school in Illinois to adopt block scheduling (extended class periods).
Unique Traits: Small class sizes, block scheduling
Public Transportation:
    CTA L: Blue Line Harlem
    Pace Bus: Harlem
    Bus: Trinity bus available at an extra cost (call school for routes)
    Metra: Geneva, Burlington
Dress Code: Uniform skirt (vote), white polo shirt
Admission Requirements: Placement exam, transcripts
Academic Scholarships: $1,200 based on placement exam

Woodlands Academy of the Sacred Heart

760 East Westleigh Road Lake Forest, IL 60045
Phone Number: (847) 234-4300
Fax Number: (847) 234-4348

Web Site: www.woodlands.lfc.edu
E-mail: admissions@woodlands.lfc.edu
Principal: Mr. Gerald Grossman, Head of School
Admissions Contact: Ms. Kathleen Creed
Gender: Girls

Total Enrollment: 175	*Student to Faculty Ratio:* 9:1
Number of Freshmen: 45	*Percentage of College Bound Grads:* 100%
Average Class Size: 15	*Tuition:* $$$$$

Other Expenditures: Yes, also general fee, boarding fee (5 or 7 days), Learning Program, English as a foreign language, and boarder's activity fee (if not available to volunteer)

Academic Specialty: College prep

Honors/Advanced Placement Classes: Yes

International Baccalaureate Program: No

Resources, Special Learning Needs: Yes, limited

Profile: Est. 1904. Day and boarding school (33% board, 13% international students). Wooded campus in upscale neighborhood. Part of worldwide network of Sacred Heart Schools. Also affiliated with the National Association of Independent Schools.

Unique Traits: Exchange program; may attend an affiliated school in U.S. or Europe

Public Transportation:
  Metra: Fort Sheridan, West Lake Forest

Dress Code: Uniform; slacks, skirt, shorts, sweater

Admission Requirements: Placement exam, transcripts, essay, interview

Academic Scholarships: $1,000 based on placement exam

Cristo Rey Jesuit High School

1852 West 22nd Place Chicago, IL 60608
Phone Number: (773) 890-6800
Fax Number: (773) 890-6801

Web Site: www.cristorey.net
E-mail: brabiela@cristorey.net
Principal: Ms. Patricia Garrity
Admissions Contact: Ms. Blanca Rabiela
Gender: Coed

Total Enrollment: 500   *Student to Faculty Ratio:* 18:1
Number of Freshmen: 160   *Percentage of College Bound Grads:* 100%
Average Class Size: 25   *Tuition:* $

Other Expenditures: Yes
Academic Specialty: College prep
Honors/Advanced Placement Classes: No
International Baccalaureate Program: No
Resources, Special Learning Needs: No
Profile: Est. 1996. Pilsen. Originally founded and still dedicated to educating children of immigrant families. Dual-language program with graduates literate in both English and Spanish.
Unique Traits: Unique corporate internship program; students earn up to 72% of their tuition by working at sponsoring Chicago corporations
Public Transportation:
     CTA L: Blue Line Hoyne
     CTA Bus: Blue Island
Dress Code: Business wear
Admission Requirements: Application, interview, low to moderate income. Must speak Spanish, be motivated and responsible, with at least a C average
Academic Scholarships: N/A

De La Salle Institute

3455 South Wabash Avenue Chicago, IL 60616
Phone Number: (312) 842-7355
Fax Number: (312) 842-5640

Web Site: www.dls.org
E-mail: kuhn@dls.org
Principal: Mr. Jim Krygier
Admissions Contact: Mr. Chuck Kuhn
Gender: Coed

Total Enrollment: 1,200   *Student to Faculty Ratio:* 17:1
Number of Freshmen: 340   *Percentage of College Bound Grads:* 95%
Average Class Size: 15–30   *Tuition:* $$

Other Expenditures: Yes
Academic Specialty: College prep
Honors/Advanced Placement Classes: Yes
International Baccalaureate Program: No
Resources, Special Learning Needs: No
Profile: Est. 1889. Bronzeville. Rooted in the tradition of St. John Baptist
     de La Salle; to educate all. Consolidated with Lourdes High School in
     2002 to form two campuses providing single gender education. Rec-
     ognized as a Blue Ribbon School.
Unique Traits: Single gender campuses are an unprecedented concept in
     Catholic education.
Public Transportation:
         CTA L: Red Line 35th, Green Line 35th
         Bus: De La Salle bus available at an extra cost (call school for
         routes)
Dress Code: Black, navy, or khaki slacks or skirt; white or blue button-
     down blouse or oxford cloth shirt
Admission Requirements: Placement exam
Academic Scholarships: $500–full tuition based on academics

Fenwick High School

505 West Washington Boulevard Oak Park, IL 60302
Phone Number: (708) 386-0127
Fax Number: (708) 386-3052

Web Site: www.fenwickfriars.com
E-mail: pvandewalle@fenwickfriars.com
Principal: Dr. James J. Quaid
Admissions Contact: Mr. Patrick Van DeWalle
Gender: Coed

Total Enrollment: 1,150   *Student to Faculty Ratio:* 16:1
Number of Freshmen: 300   *Percentage of College Bound Grads:* 100%
Average Class Size: 17   *Tuition:* $$$

Other Expenditures: Yes
Academic Specialty: College prep
Honors/Advanced Placement Classes: Yes
International Baccalaureate Program: No
Resources, Special Learning Needs: No
Profile: Est. 1929. In the Dominican tradition; religious and cultural heritage in a Christian atmosphere. An exemplary U.S. Department of Education School Design. Listed in *U.S. News & World Report*'s "96 Outstanding American High Schools," January 1999. Recognized as a Blue Ribbon School.
Unique Traits: Draws students from 27 different suburbs
Public Transportation:
   Bus: Fenwick bus available at an extra cost (call school for routes)
   Metra: River Grove
Dress Code: Boys: dress slacks, button-down shirt, tie, dress shoes. Girls: uniform skirt, blouse or turtleneck, dress shoes
Admission Requirements: Placement exam
Academic Scholarships: $1,500 each year based on placement exam

Gordon Tech High School

3633 North California Avenue Chicago, IL 60618
Phone Number: (773) 539-3600
Fax Number: (773) 539-9158

Web Site: www.gordontech.org
E-mail: pchabura@gordontech.org
Principal: William Watts, PhD
Admissions Contact: Mr. Paul Chabura
Gender: Coed

Total Enrollment: 590   *Student to Faculty Ratio:* 17:1
Number of Freshmen: 145   *Percentage of College Bound Grads:* 85%
Average Class Size: 26   *Tuition:* $$

Other Expenditures: Yes
Academic Specialty: College prep
Honors/Advanced Placement Classes: Yes
International Baccalaureate Program: No
Resources, Special Learning Needs: No
Profile: Est. 1952. North side. Known for its racial and ethnic diversity and strong sense of community. One of the largest libraries in the Chicago Catholic high school system. Member of the National Consortium of High Schools.
Unique Traits: State-of-the-art technology lab, first of its kind in any Chicago Catholic high school
Public Transportation:
    CTA L: Red Line Addison, Blue Line Addison
    CTA Bus: Addison, California
Dress Code: Khaki slacks or skort, school polo shirt or blouse
Admission Requirements: Placement exam, minimum C average in 8th grade
Academic Scholarships: $500, $1,000 based on placement exam

Guerin College Preparatory High School

8001 West Belmont Avenue River Grove, IL 60171
Phone Number: (708) 453-6233
Fax Number: (708) 453-6296

Web Site: www.guerinprep.org
E-mail: vreiss@guerinprep.org
Principal: Ms. Bonnie Brown
Admissions Contact: Ms. Valerie Reiss
Gender: Coed

Total Enrollment: 730   *Student/Faculty Ratio:* 12:1
Number of Freshmen: 210   *Percentage of College Bound Grads:* 96%
Class Size: 24   *Tuition:* $$

Other Expenditures: Yes, plus registration fee
Academic Specialty: College Prep
Honors/Advanced Placement Classes: Yes
International Baccalaureate Program: No
Resources, Special Learning Needs: No
Profile: Est. 1962. Since the closing of nearby Holy Cross (a Catholic boys
   school), Guerin has acquired their 14 acres of buildings and grounds
   (to add to its 10-acre campus) and has become a coed school.
Unique Traits: Extensive fine arts department
Public Transportation:
   CTA Bus: Pacific
   Pace Bus: Cumberland
Dress Code: Black or khaki Dockers, each class wears different color
   school polo shirt
Admission Requirements: Placement exam, transcripts, teacher
   recommendations
Academic Scholarships: $1,500–$2,000 based on placement exam (renew-
   able for sophomore year with certain restrictions)

Holy Trinity High School

1443 West Division Street Chicago, IL 60622
Phone Number: (773) 278-4212
Fax Number: (773) 278-0729

Web Site: www.holytrinity-hs.org
E-mail: mstratman@holytrinity-hs.org
Principal: Ms. Charlene Szumilas
Admissions Contact: Ms. Melinda Stratman
Gender: Coed

Total Enrollment: 420   *Student to Faculty Ratio:* 14:1
Number of Freshmen: 135   *Percentage of College Bound Grads:* 95%
Average Class Size: 15–20   *Tuition:* $$

Other Expenditures: Yes, also fundraising
Academic Specialty: College prep
Honors/Advanced Placement Classes: Yes
International Baccalaureate Program: No
Resources, Special Learning Needs: Yes
Profile: Est. 1910. Wicker Park/Bucktown. Diverse student population. Block scheduling. Only Catholic high school to offer Upward Bound, a federally funded tutoring/enrichment program for low-income students.
Unique Traits: Corporate internships, Upward Bound Program
Public Transportation:
>   CTA L: Blue Line Division
>   CTA Bus: Division, Ashland, Milwaukee
Dress Code: Solid color slacks or skirt, school polo shirt, sweatshirt, or sweater
Admission Requirements: Placement exam
Academic Scholarships: $2,500 if above 85% based on placement exam

Loyola Academy

1100 Laramie Avenue Wilmette, IL 60091
Phone Number: (847) 256-1100
Fax Number: (847) 853-4512

Web Site: www.goramblers.org
E-mail: lseitzinger@loy.org
Principal: Mr. Dave McNulty
Admissions Contact: Mr. Les Seitzinger
Gender: Coed

Total Enrollment: 2,000   *Student to Faculty Ratio:* 17:1
Number of Freshmen: 530   *Percentage of College Bound Grads:* 99%
Average Class Size: 23   *Tuition:* $$$

Other Expenditures: Yes
Academic Specialty: College prep
Honors/Advanced Placement Classes: Yes
International Baccalaureate Program: No
Resources, Special Learning Needs: Yes
Profile: Est. 1909. Traditional. Liberal arts education with strong spiritual
    side. Athletic fields located on 60-acre Glenview campus. One of the
    nation's most respected schools.
Unique Traits: College prep in the Jesuit tradition
Public Transportation:
        CTA L: Purple Line Linden
        Metra: Wilmette
Dress Code: Slacks (no skirts), shirt or blouse with collar
Admission Requirements: Placement exam, transcripts
Academic Scholarships: N/A

Marist High School

4200 West 115th Street Chicago, IL 60655
Phone Number: (773) 881-6300
Fax Number: (773) 881-0595

Web Site: www.marist.net
E-mail: alex@marist.net
Principal: Mr. Larry Tucker
Admissions Contact: Ms. Alexandra Brown
Gender: Coed

Total Enrollment: 1,829	*Student to Faculty Ratio:* 16:1
Number of Freshmen: 485	*Percentage of College Bound Grads:* 100%
Average Class Size: 29	*Tuition:* $$

Other Expenditures: Yes
Academic Specialty: College prep
Honors/Advanced Placement Classes: Yes
International Baccalaureate Program: No
Resources, Special Learning Needs: Yes
Profile: Est. 1963. Southwest side. 55-acre campus. Rooted in the spirit of the Marist Brothers. Personalized student programs to promote critical thinking skills.
Unique Traits: One of the top computer programs in Illinois
Public Transportation:
> CTA L: Orange Line Kedzie
> CTA Bus: Kedzie
> Bus: Marist bus available at an extra cost (call school for routes)

Dress Code: Slacks, skirt, button-down shirt (Friday: school polo shirt)
Admission Requirements: Placement exam, transcripts
Academic Scholarships: Based on placement exam: $500–$1,500

Nazareth Academy

1209 West Ogden Avenue La Grange Park, IL 60526
Phone Number: (708) 354-0061
Fax Number: (708) 354-0109

Web Site: www.nazarethacademy.com
E-mail: tmmidden@nazarethacademy.com
Principal: Ms. Deborah A. Vondrasek
Admissions Contact: Sr. Therese Middendorf, CSJ
Gender: Coed

Total Enrollment: 765   *Student to Faculty Ratio:* 17:1
Number of Freshmen: 210   *Percentage of College Bound Grads:* 100%
Average Class Size: 24   *Tuition:* $$$

Other Expenditures: Yes
Academic Specialty: College prep
Honors/Advanced Placement Classes: Yes
International Baccalaureate Program: No
Resources, Special Learning Needs: No
Profile: Est. 1900. Western suburbs. Founded and sponsored by the Sisters of St. Joseph. Traditional. Strong emphasis on academics, service, and the development of the whole person.
Unique Traits: Serves students in over 45 communities
Public Transportation:
> *Pace Bus:* LaGrange
> *Bus:* Nazareth bus available at an extra cost (call school for routes)
> *Metra:* LaGrange

Dress Code: Boys: Docker slacks, shirt, tie (school polo shirt on Fridays). Girls: uniform slacks or skirt, blouse or school polo shirt
Admission Requirements: Placement exam, transcripts
Academic Scholarships: $1,000 based on academic performance, leadership, community/school service

St. Benedict High School

3900 North Leavitt Street Chicago, IL 60618
Phone Number: (773) 539-0066
Fax Number: (773) 539-3397

Web Site: www.stbenedict.com
E-mail: mknickels@stbenedict.com
Principal: Ms. Mary Kay Nickels
Admissions Contact: Ms. Elizabeth Shriner
Gender: Coed

Total Enrollment: 1,000   *Student to Faculty Ratio:* 15:1
Number of Freshmen: 72   *Percentage of College Bound Grads:* 90%
Average Class Size: 22   *Tuition:* $$

Other Expenditures: Yes
Academic Specialty: College prep
Honors/Advanced Placement Classes: Yes
International Baccalaureate Program: No
Resources, Special Learning Needs: Yes
Profile: Est. 1950. North side. Grades K–12. Economically, ethnically, and racially diverse. Recent endowment responsible for new 3-story building. A DePaul University Professional Development Partner School.
Unique Traits: One of only three archdiocese high schools on the same street with its parish elementary school
Public Transportation:
      CTA L: Brown Line Irving Park
      CTA Bus: Irving Park, Damen, Western, Addison
Dress Code: Brown, blue, or khaki slacks; school polo shirt
Admission Requirements: Placement exam, transcripts
Academic Scholarships: Based on placement exam

St. Francis de Sales High School

10155 South Ewing Avenue Chicago, IL 60617
Phone Number: (773) 731-7272
Fax Number: (773) 731-7888

Web Site: www.sfdshs.org
E-mail: jboyle@sfdshs.org
Principal: Mr. Richard Hawkins
Admissions Contact: Mr. John Boyle
Gender: Coed

Total Enrollment: 365   *Student to Faculty Ratio:* 14:1
Number of Freshmen: 125   *Percentage of College Bound Grads:* 90%
Average Class Size: 18–22   *Tuition:* $$

Other Expenditures: Yes, also fundraising
Academic Specialty: College prep
Honors/Advanced Placement Classes: Yes
International Baccalaureate Program: No
Resources, Special Learning Needs: No
Profile: Est. 1893. East side. Small school with very diverse student population. Committed to Christian education for over 100 years.
Unique Traits: Chicago's oldest coed Catholic high school.
Public Transportation:
    CTA Bus: 102nd, Ewing
Dress Code: Black, navy, or khaki slacks or skirt; school polo shirt; school sweater
Admission Requirements: Placement exam, transcripts, teacher recommendations
Academic Scholarships: Based on placement exam

St. Gregory High School

1677 West Bryn Mawr Avenue Chicago, IL 60660
Phone Number: (773) 907-2100
Fax Number: (773) 907-2120

Web Site: www.stgregory.org
E-mail: info@stgregory.org
Principal: Ms. Erika Mickelburgh
Admissions Contact: Mr. Titus Redmond
Gender: Coed

Total Enrollment: 205	*Student to Faculty Ratio:* 11:1
Number of Freshmen: 50	*Percentage of College Bound Grads:* 80%
Average Class Size: 15	*Tuition:* $$

Other Expenditures: Yes
Academic Specialty: College prep
Honors/Advanced Placement Classes: Yes
International Baccalaureate Program: No
Resources, Special Learning Needs: Yes
Profile: Est. 1937. Edgewater. Small student population. Custom curriculum planning to assist students with a wide range of abilities. Secure and caring environment. Dance and theater classes at nearby studios.
Unique Traits: Protégé Internship Program, block scheduling, Homeroom Houses (information and activities with a mix of classes)
Public Transportation:
    CTA L: Red Line Bryn Mawr
    CTA Bus: Damen
Dress Code: Khaki slacks, school polo shirt, brown or black shoes
Admission Requirements: Placement exam
Academic Scholarships: N/A

St. Ignatius College Prep High School

1076 West Roosevelt Road Chicago, IL 60608
Phone Number: (312) 421-5900
Fax Number: (312) 421-7124

Web Site: www.ignatius.org
E-mail: claire.larmon@ignatius.org
Principal: Dr. Catherine A. Karl
Admissions Contact: Ms. Claire Larmon
Gender: Coed

Total Enrollment: 1,370   *Student to Faculty Ratio:* 16:1
Number of Freshmen: 350   *Percentage of College Bound Grads:* 99%
Average Class Size: 24   *Tuition:* $$$

Other Expenditures: Yes, also parent pledge
Academic Specialty: College prep
Honors/Advanced Placement Classes: Yes
International Baccalaureate Program: No
Resources, Special Learning Needs: No
Profile: Est. 1870. West side. Founded by the Society of Jesus. Demanding curriculum in the classical Jesuit tradition. 19-acre campus. National Historic Landmark building. Known as one of the most prestigious high schools in Chicago.
Unique Traits: Draw students from over 300 city and suburban grade schools
Public Transportation:
    CTA L: Blue Line Halsted
    CTA Bus: Halsted, Roosevelt
    Metra: LaSalle, Union; Ignatius shuttle available from Metra stations at an extra cost
Dress Code: Slacks or skirt (no denim), shirt with collar and sleeves
Admission Requirements: Placement exam, transcripts
Academic Scholarships: N/A

St. Joseph High School

1840 South Mayfair Avenue Westchester, IL 60154
Phone Number: (708) 562-4433
Fax Number: (708) 562-4459

Web Site: www.stjoeshs.org
E-mail: jtortorich@stjoeshs.org
Principal: Ms. Donna Kiel
Admissions Contact: Mr. Joe Tortorich
Gender: Coed

Total Enrollment: 775   *Student to Faculty Ratio:* 22:1
Number of Freshmen: 215   *Percentage of College Bound Grads:* 98%
Average Class Size: 24   *Tuition:* $$

Other Expenditures: Yes, also raffle tickets, laptop computer
Academic Specialty: College prep
Honors/Advanced Placement Classes: Yes
International Baccalaureate Program: No
Resources, Special Learning Needs: No
Profile: Est. 1960. Coed in 2005. Follows the practices and teachings of St. John Baptist De La Salle. Extremely diverse and accepting of students at all academic levels. Received the highest curriculum endorsement through the North Central Association.
Unique Traits: Every student has their own laptop (wireless Internet throughout building)
Public Transportation:
    Pace Bus: Mayfair
Dress Code: Boys: black, navy, or gray dress slacks; white or light blue dress shirt; dress shoes. Girls: plaid skirt, khaki slacks, school polo shirt
Admission Requirements: Placement exam
Academic Scholarships: $250–$1,000 based on placement exam

St. Viator High School

1213 East Oakton Arlington Heights, IL 60004
Phone Number: (847) 392-4050
Fax Number: (847) 392-4329

Web Site: www.saintviator.com
E-mail: bealion@saintviator.com
Principal: Rev. Robert M. Egan, CSV, President
Admissions Contact: Ms. Melissa Strzelinski
Gender: Coed

Total Enrollment: 1,040   *Student to Faculty Ratio:* 13:1
Number of Freshmen: 265   *Percentage of College Bound Grads:* 99%
Average Class Size: 25   *Tuition:* $$$

Other Expenditures: Yes, also nonrefundable tuition deposit
Academic Specialty: College prep
Honors/Advanced Placement Classes: Yes
International Baccalaureate Program: No
Resources, Special Learning Needs: Yes
Profile: Est. 1961. Founded by Fr. Louis Querbes in the Viatorian tradition; a lifelong journey of spiritual and learning development ("viatorian" means traveler).
Unique Traits: Academic excellence in a family atmosphere
Public Transportation:
     Metra: Arlington Heights, complimentary shuttle bus available
Dress Code: Khaki, black, navy, green, or gray slacks, shorts, skirt, or skort; dress shirt, school polo shirt, or sweatshirt
Admission Requirements: Placement exam, interview, transcripts, teacher evaluation
Academic Scholarships: Based on placement exam

Seton Academy

16100 South Seton Road South Holland, IL 60473
Phone Number: (708) 333-6300
Fax Number: (708) 333-1534

Web Site: www.seton-academy.org
E-mail: See Web site
Principal: Ms. Mary Iannucilli
Admissions Contact: Ms. Kerry Griffin
Gender: Coed

Total Enrollment: 375 *Student to Faculty Ratio:* 18:1
Number of Freshmen: 165 *Percentage of College Bound Grads:* 99%
Average Class Size: 18–25 *Tuition:* $$

Other Expenditures: Yes
Academic Specialty: College prep
Honors/Advanced Placement Classes: Yes
International Baccalaureate Program: No
Resources, Special Learning Needs: No
Profile: Est. 1963. Diverse, antiracist learning community. Holistic
approach to education based on values and faith.
Unique Traits: Nurturing developmental approach
Public Transportation:
    Pace Bus: 159th
Dress Code: Neutral slacks, plaid skirt
Admission Requirements: Placement exam, transcripts
Academic Scholarships: Based on placement exam

A Uniform Decision

A Catholic Coed High School Experience

By L.P.

My son is a stick-to-the-rules kind of guy. Ever since he was a little boy, he's liked to have the parameters set and then work within them. For this reason, even though we are not Catholic, we chose a Catholic grammar school for him. It was his kind of place from the start. But when it came time to look at high schools, I felt we should be open to other possibilities and to really see what was available. As it turned out, one Sunday afternoon of open-house visits put it all in perspective for our family.

Our first stop of the day was to one of the premier Catholic high schools. Classic in style, its historic buildings and years of academic excellence were impressive. Students dressed in their Sunday best escorted families on tours. Yes, I could definitely envision my son walking through these hallowed halls, but could he?

Next, we visited one of the best new public schools. It was a state-of-the-art facility, contemporary in its design and, yes, also impressive, but it was as different from the first school as night and day. The student who gave us our tour had multiple body piercings. A demonstration of a mock class showed jean-clad students with their bare feet on the table debating current events, their level of conversation rivaling any college classroom's.

Ambience aside, each of these schools offered excellent opportunities in its own right. Each boasted a rigorous academic program, was coed and equidistant from our home, and only accepted the crème de la crème (translation: not easy to get into).

As you can probably guess, the Catholic school was my son's first choice (his backups were also Catholic coed schools) and he's now thriving in what is the perfect atmosphere for him. He's fine with the fact that he'll get detention if his shirt is untucked. He's comfortable not walking up the down staircase. He's happy that all the students dress for dances, rather than showing up in pajama pants and flip-flops.

Don't get me wrong—I am not praising one school's style over another. I am just making the point that you have to take the time to see what's out there and then steer your child accordingly. There are as many choices as there are personalities and, believe me, if you give this project the time and energy it deserves, you will receive the gift of seeing your child content in the high school environment he or she is best suited for.

Independent High Schools

Introduction

The National Association of Independent Schools is an organization of nine hundred schools across the country. These schools are privately supported and are not dependent on public or church funds. They must meet certain criteria and maintain high standards as members of regional and national independent agencies.

Students must preregister to take the Independent School Entrance Exam (ISEE). Applicants should call the Educational Records Bureau (ERB) at (800) 989-3721 to receive an ISEE guide. Testing dates are from November–February. Choose the most convenient date and testing location; test location does not affect school choice. The test is three hours long. Admission decisions are mailed on or around March 1.

When reviewing independent school options, look for special designations and awards given to schools. *U.S. News & World Report* and the *Chicago Sun-Times* included some of the area's independent high schools in their reports of outstanding high schools.

Independent schools offer a wide variety of curriculum options. These private institutions can be large and prestigious or small and experimental and include military boarding schools (boys and coed), boarding schools, and nontraditional settings based on a particular philosophy or centered on the arts.

Since every school offers financial aid, no separate heading for it appears in the individual school listings. There are literally millions of dollars made available each year to those students who qualify.

High school fairs offer a way to obtain an overview of many schools, which may entice you to plan a visit or to give a school a second look. For timely information on independent high school fairs, log on to www.info@independent schools.net.

Independent High Schools: Boys

Independent High Schools: Girls

Independent High Schools: Coed

Northridge Prep School

8320 Ballard Road Niles, IL 60714
Phone Number: (847) 375-0600
Fax Number: (847) 375-0606

Web Site: www.northridgeprep.org
E-mail: csullivan@northridgeprep.org
Principal: Mr. Luke Ferris
Admissions Contact: Mr. Charles W. Sullivan
Gender: Boys

Total Enrollment: 300   *Student to Faculty Ratio:* 10:1
Number of Freshmen: 50   *Percentage of College Bound Grads:* 100%
Average Class Size: 22   *Tuition:* $$$

Other Expenditures: Yes
Academic Specialty: College prep
Honors/Advanced Placement Classes: Yes
International Baccalaureate Program: No
Resources, Special Learning Needs: No
Profile: Est. 1975. Grades 6–12. Inspired by the teachings of the Catholic Church and the spirituality of the Prelature of Opus Dei. One of the fastest growing Chicago area schools. Named "One of the Top Ten Chicago Schools" by the *Chicago Sun-Times*. Listed in *U.S. News & World Report*'s "96 Outstanding American High Schools," January 1999.
Unique Traits: Approved by the archdiocese to teach Catholic theology (optional for non-Catholics)
Public Transportation:
   Pace Bus: Milwaukee, Evanston-Niles, Golf-Woodfield, Glenview-O'Hare
   Bus: Northridge bus available from Metra station at an extra cost
   Metra: Des Plaines, Morton Grove
Dress Code: Blue slacks, blue blazer, white or blue shirt, tie
Admission Requirements: Transcripts (grades, test scores)
Academic Scholarships: N/A

St. John's Northwestern Military Academy

1101 North Genesee Street Delafield, WI 53018
Phone Number: (262) 646-7199
Fax Number: (262) 646-7128

Web Site: www.sjnma.com
E-mail: admissions@sjnma.com
Principal: Mr. Jack H. Albert, Jr., President
Admissions Contact: Mr. Charles E. Moore
Gender: Boys

Total Enrollment: 300	*Student to Faculty Ratio:* 12:1
Number of Freshmen: 65	*Percentage of College Bound Grads:* 100%
Average Class Size: 12	*Tuition:* $$$$$ includes room and board

Other Expenditures: Yes, also a one time uniform fee
Academic Specialty: College prep
Honors/Advanced Placement Classes: Yes
International Baccalaureate Program: No
Resources, Special Learning Needs: Yes
Profile: Est. 1884. Military boarding school. Small class sizes. Supervised study halls. Compulsory sports. Mandatory chapel. Students develop character, manners, and values and earn time-management skills and self-discipline. JROTC program is an Honor Unit with Distinction providing leadership opportunities.
Unique Traits: Military boarding school.
Public Transportation: N/A
Dress Code: Military uniform
Admission Requirements: Placement exam, transcripts, interview
Academic Scholarships: Academic Excellence and Old Boy Alumni Association Scholarships

Willows Academy

1012 Thacker Street Des Plaines, IL 60018
Phone Number: (847) 824-6900
Fax Number: (847) 824-7089

Web Site: www.willows.org
E-mail: info@willows.org
Principal: Ms. Tina Verhelst
Admissions Contact: Ms. Dorothy Boland
Gender: Girls

Total Enrollment: 215   *Student to Faculty Ratio:* 12:1
Number of Freshmen: 50   *Percentage of College Bound Grads:* 100%
Average Class Size: 18   *Tuition:* $$$$$ includes room and board

Other Expenditures: Yes, also computer fee
Academic Specialty: College prep
Honors/Advanced Placement Classes: Yes
International Baccalaureate Program: No
Resources, Special Learning Needs: No
Profile: Est. 1974. Grades 6–12. Inspired by the teachings of the Catholic Church and spirituality of the Prelature of Opus Dei. Ethnically and racially diverse. Draws students from over 50 Chicago communities.
Unique Traits: Approved by the archdiocese to teach Catholic theology (optional for non-Catholics)
Public Transportation:
> *Pace Bus:* Golf-Woodfield, Glenview-O'Hare, Evanston-Des Plaines, S. Des Plaines
> *Metra:* Des Plaines
Dress Code: Plaid skirt, school polo shirt, sweater, or sweatshirt
Admission Requirements: Entrance exam, application, transcripts, interview
Academic Scholarships: No

British School of Chicago

1643 West Bryn Mawr Avenue Chicago, IL 60660
Phone Number: (773) 506-2097
Fax Number: (773) 506-4805

Web Site: www.britishschoolchicago.org
E-mail: admissionsbsc@britishschool.org
Principal: Mr. Michael Horton
Admissions Contact: Ms. Anne Newman
Gender: Coed

Total Enrollment: 180	*Student to Faculty Ratio:* 10:1
Number of Freshmen: N/A	*Percentage of College Bound Grads:* 100%
Average Class Size: 20	*Tuition:* $$$

Other Expenditures: Yes
Academic Specialty: College prep
Honors/Advanced Placement Classes: No
International Baccalaureate Program: No
Resources, Special Learning Needs: No
Profile: Est. 2001. Andersonville. Grades Pre-K–12 (high school opened September 2005). Challenging curriculum based on the UK National & International Primary Curriculum. Specialist teaching in music, sports, and French.
Unique Traits: International education, individual programs
Public Transportation:
   CTA Bus: Ashland
Dress Code: Navy slacks or skirt, white shirt, navy school sweater
Admission Requirements: Transcripts. Open enrollment: students accepted throughout the year if space is available
Academic Scholarships: No

Chicago Academy for the Arts

1010 West Chicago Avenue Chicago, IL 60622
Phone Number: (312) 421-0202
Fax Number: (312) 421-3816

Web Site: www.chicagoacademyforthearts.org
E-mail: admissions@chicagoacademyforthearts.org
Principal: Ms. Pamela Jordan
Admissions Contact: Mr. Mark Taylor
Gender: Coed

Total Enrollment: 150	*Student to Faculty Ratio:* 10:1
Number of Freshmen: 40	*Percentage of College Bound Grads:* N/A
Average Class Size: 10–20	*Tuition:* $$$$$

Other Expenditures: Yes, also private lesson fees
Academic Specialty: College prep
Honors/Advanced Placement Classes: Yes
International Baccalaureate Program: No
Resources, Special Learning Needs: Yes
Profile: Est. 1980. River West. Nontraditional setting for the talented student. Mornings: fully accredited college prep classes. Afternoon: focus on art form including history, theory, and technique. Creative facilities include art, dance, and music studios, art gallery, and theater.
Unique Traits: One of five private arts high schools in the country
Public Transportation:
> *CTA L:* Blue Line Chicago
> *CTA Bus:* Carpenter
> *Bus:* Complimentary school shuttle from Northwestern, Union, and LaSalle train stations
Dress Code: Appropriate casual; jeans acceptable
Admission Requirements: Scholastic ability (entrance exam, transcripts), artistic evaluation (audition or portfolio), interview
Academic Scholarships: Merit scholarship based on recommendation, transcripts, and written essay

Chicago Waldorf School

130 West Loyola Avenue Chicago, IL 60626
Phone Number: (773) 465-2662
Fax Number: (773) 465-6648

Web Site: www.chicagowaldorf.org
E-mail: info@chicagowaldorf.org
Principal: Ms. Colleen Everhart, High School Chairperson
Admissions Contact: Ms. Phyllis Marder
Gender: Coed

Total Enrollment: 350   *Student to Faculty Ratio:* 6:1
Number of Freshmen: 18   *Percentage of College Bound Grads:* 90%
Average Class Size: 15–26   *Tuition:* $$$$

Other Expenditures: Yes, also application fee, supply fee, service learning fee, and Association of Waldorf Schools dues
Academic Specialty: College prep
Honors/Advanced Placement Classes: No
International Baccalaureate Program: No
Resources, Special Learning Needs: Yes, limited
Profile: Est. 1974. Rogers Park. Grades Pre-K–12. Largest nondenominational educational movement in the world; 800 schools in 35 countries. Based on a multisensory approach to learning that stresses imagination. No formal textbooks. Focus is not on computer use or testing.
Unique Traits: Unique learning approach: balance between academics, arts, and practical learning
Public Transportation:
       CTA L: Red Line Loyola
       CTA Bus: Sheridan
Dress Code: Jeans acceptable, appropriate casual
Admission Requirements: Application, transcripts, parent/student interview, math and reading assessment
Academic Scholarships: No

Howe Military School

5755 North S.R.9 (P.O. Box 240) Howe, IN 46746
Phone Number: (260) 562-2131
Fax Number: (260) 562-3678

Web Site: www.howemilitary.com
E-mail: admissions@howemilitary.com
Principal: Mr. James Malerich, Headmaster
Admissions Contact: Dr. Brent Smith
Gender: Coed

Total Enrollment: 150　　*Student to Faculty Ratio:* 6:1
Number of Freshmen: 25　　*Percentage of College Bound Grads:* 97%
Average Class Size: 10　　*Tuition:* $$$$$ includes room and board

Other Expenditures: Yes, also computer lease fee
Academic Specialty: College prep (no ROTC)
Honors/Advanced Placement Classes: Yes
International Baccalaureate Program: No
Resources, Special Learning Needs: No
Profile: Est. 1884. Grades 5–12. Military boarding school on 100 rural acres. Students come from 17 states and several countries. Unique individual grading system. The St. James Chapel and Howe Mansion are on the National Historic Register.
Unique Traits: Very structured, strict atmosphere
Public Transportation: N/A
Dress Code: Military uniform
Admission Requirements: Entrance exam, transcripts, teacher references, student/parent tour
Academic Scholarships: Based on transcripts

Lake Forest Academy

1500 West Kennedy Road Lake Forest, IL 60045
Phone Number: (847) 615-3267
Fax Number: (847) 615-3202

Web Site: www.lfanet.org
E-mail: info@lfanet.org
Principal: Dr. John Strudwick, Head of School
Admissions Contact: Ms. Karen Cegelski
Gender: Coed

Total Enrollment: 370   *Student to Faculty Ratio:* 7:1
Number of Freshmen: 80   *Percentage of College Bound Grads:* 100%
Average Class Size: 12   *Tuition:* $$$$$ with or without room/board

Other Expenditures: Yes
Academic Specialty: College prep
Honors/Advanced Placement Classes: Yes
International Baccalaureate Program: No
Resources, Special Learning Needs: No
Profile: Est. 1857. Boarding and day school (50% board). Former 160-acre
    estate of J. Ogden Armour. Affluent neighborhood. Traditional, rigor-
    ous academic program. Performing and fine arts programs.
Unique Traits: Students come from 15 countries and 20 states
Public Transportation:
    Metra: Lake Forest, complimentary shuttle bus
Dress Code: Dress slacks, dress, skirt, button-down shirt, tie, blouse. No
    denim or sneakers.
Admission Requirements: Entrance exam, transcripts, application
Academic Scholarships: $4,000–$6,000 merit grants based on exam and
    transcripts

La Lumiere School

6801 North Wilhelm Road LaPorte, IN 46350
Phone Number: (219) 326-7450
Fax Number: (219) 325-3185

Web Site: www.lalumiere.org
E-mail: admissions@lalumiere.org
Principal: Mr. Michael Kennedy, Headmaster
Admissions Contact: Ms. Melissa Machaj
Gender: Coed

Total Enrollment: 120
Student to Faculty Ratio: 6:1
Number of Freshmen: 20
Percentage of College Bound Grads: 100%
Average Class Size: 12
Tuition: $$$$$ with or without room/board

Other Expenditures: Yes, also technology, yearbook, and graduation fees
Academic Specialty: College prep
Honors/Advanced Placement Classes: Yes
International Baccalaureate Program: No
Resources, Special Learning Needs: No
Profile: Est. 1963. Boarding and day school. 60 miles east of Chicago. Wooded 155-acre campus with 35-acre lake. Student body is composed of approximately 15% international students.
Unique Traits: Cross-curricular writing program and award-winning art department
Public Transportation: N/A
Dress Code: Gray or navy slacks or skirt; solid color, collared shirt; navy blazer; tie
Admission Requirements: Application, interview
Academic Scholarships: Yes

Latin School of Chicago

59 West North Avenue Chicago, IL 60610
Phone Number: (312) 582-6060
Fax Number: (312) 582-6061

Web Site: www.latinschool.org
E-mail: info@latinschool.org
Principal: Mr. Donald Firke
Admissions Contact: Ms. Anne Frame
Gender: Coed

Total Enrollment: 1,080   *Student to Faculty Ratio:* 20:1
Number of Freshmen: 115   *Percentage of College Bound Grads:* 100%
Average Class Size: 20   *Tuition:* $$$$$

Other Expenditures: Yes, also Capital Campaign donation, voluntary support fund
Academic Specialty: College prep
Honors/Advanced Placement Classes: Yes
International Baccalaureate Program: No
Resources, Special Learning Needs: Yes
Profile: Est. 1888. North side. Grades Junior-K–12. Separate building for middle and high school. Prestigious. Traditional and rigorous academic program.
Unique Traits: Oldest independent day school in Chicago
Public Transportation:
   CTA L: Brown Line Sedgwick, Red Line Clark/Division
   CTA Bus: Clark, LaSalle, Broadway, Lincoln, North
Dress Code: Appropriate casual; jeans acceptable
Admission Requirements: Entrance exam, application, transcripts, principal and teacher recommendations. Preference is given to siblings and children of alumni
Academic Scholarships: No

Morgan Park Academy

2153 West 111th Street Chicago, IL 60643
Phone Number: (773) 881-6700
Fax Number: (773) 881-8409

Web Site: www.morganparkacademy.org
E-mail: mharmening@morganparkacademy.org
Principal: Mr. David Hibbs
Admissions Contact: Ms. Melissa Harmening
Gender: Coed

Total Enrollment: 545   *Student to Faculty Ratio:* 10:1
Number of Freshmen: 50   *Percentage of College Bound Grads:* 100%
Average Class Size: 5–18   *Tuition:* $$$$

Other Expenditures: Yes
Academic Specialty: College prep
Honors/Advanced Placement Classes: Yes
International Baccalaureate Program: No
Resources, Special Learning Needs: No
Profile: Est. 1873. Beverly/Morgan Park. Grades Junior-K–12. 20-acre Ivy League campus. Multicultural and socioeconomic student mix. Hands-on approach with emphasis on the individual. Named "One of the Top Ten Chicago High Schools" by the *Chicago Sun-Times.*
Unique Traits: Over the national average in National Merit competitions in the past 5 years
Public Transportation:
   Metra: 111th, Western
Dress Code: Appropriate casual; jeans acceptable
Admission Requirements: Entrance exam, recommendations
Academic Scholarships: Up to 50% off all 4 years based on exam and transcripts

North Shore Country Day School

310 Green Bay Road Winnetka, IL 60093
Phone Number: (847) 441-3313
Fax Number: (847) 446-0675

Web Site: www.aboutnscds.org
E-mail: dwentz@nscds.org
Principal: Mr. Tom Doar
Admissions Contact: Ms. Dale Wentz
Gender: Coed

Total Enrollment: 450   *Student to Faculty Ratio:* 8:1
Number of Freshmen: 45   *Percentage of College Bound Grads:* 100%
Average Class Size: 15   *Tuition:* $$$$$

Other Expenditures: Yes
Academic Specialty: College prep
Honors/Advanced Placement Classes: Yes
International Baccalaureate Program: No
Resources, Special Learning Needs: Yes
Profile: Est. 1919. Grades Junior-K–12. Located on 16 acres. Independent study courses; opportunities to lead
Unique Traits: State-of-the-art Science Center
Public Transportation:
          Metra: Winnetka
Dress Code: Appropriate casual; jeans acceptable
Admission Requirements: Entrance exam, transcripts, teacher recommendations, day visit
Academic Scholarships: Based on exam, transcripts, teacher recommendations, interview

Francis W. Parker School

330 West Webster Avenue Chicago, IL 60614
Phone Number: (773) 353-3000
Fax Number: (773) 549-0587

Web Site: www.fwparker.org
E-mail: info@fwparker.org
Principal: Dr. Daniel B. Frank
Admissions Contact: Ms. Cokey Evans
Gender: Coed

Total Enrollment: 910   *Student to Faculty Ratio:* 8:1
Number of Freshmen: 80   *Percentage of College Bound Grads:* 100%
Average Class Size: 18   *Tuition:* $$$$$

Other Expenditures: Yes, also application fee, class fees, Fair Share annual
contribution
Academic Specialty: College prep
Honors/Advanced Placement Classes: Yes
International Baccalaureate Program: No
Resources, Special Learning Needs: Yes
Profile: Est. 1901. Lincoln Park. Grades Junior-K–12. Founded by Colonel
Francis Parker and based on John Dewey's educational theory of com-
plete mental, physical, and moral development of the individual.
Unique Traits: A progressive school promoting resourcefulness and
creativity
Public Transportation:
    CTA L: Fullerton
    CTA Bus: Clark, LaSalle, Broadway, Sheridan
Dress Code: Appropriate casual; jeans acceptable
Admission Requirements: Application, entrance exam, transcripts, princi-
pal and teacher recommendations, interview
Academic Scholarships: No

Roycemore School

640 Lincoln Street Evanston, IL 60201
Phone Number: (847) 866-6055
Fax Number: (847) 866-6545

Web Site: www.roycemoreschool.org
E-mail: info@roycemoreschool.org
Principal: Mr. Frank Spica, Principal, Upper School
Admissions Contact: Ms. Barbara Turnbull
Gender: Coed

Total Enrollment: 250	*Student to Faculty Ratio:* 8:1
Number of Freshmen: 25	*Percentage of College Bound Grads:* 100%
Average Class Size: 5–18	*Tuition:* $$$$$

Other Expenditures: Yes, also supplies
Academic Specialty: College prep
Honors/Advanced Placement Classes: Yes
International Baccalaureate Program: No
Resources, Special Learning Needs: Yes
Profile: Est. 1915. Grades Pre-K–12. National Historic Register building. Course affiliation with Northwestern University. January term is shortened for independent student projects at school, in the area, or the world.
Unique Traits: Small class size, personal attention
Public Transportation:
      CTA L: Purple Line Noyes
      CTA Bus: Sherman
Dress Code: Appropriate casual; jeans acceptable
Admission Requirements: No entrance exam; transcripts, writing sample
Academic Scholarships: Full tuition based on recommendation, transcripts, 95th percentile rank

University of Chicago Laboratory School

1362 East 59th Street Chicago, IL 60637
Phone Number: (773) 702-9450
Fax Number: (773) 702-7455

Web Site: www.ucls.uchicago.edu
E-mail: admissions@ucls.uchicago.edu
Principal: Mr. Jack Knapp
Admissions Contact: Mr. Michael Veitch
Gender: Coed

Total Enrollment: 1,715   *Student to Faculty Ratio:* 10:1
Number of Freshmen: 125   *Percentage of College Bound Grads:* 100%
Average Class Size: 20   *Tuition:* $$$$$

Other Expenditures: Yes, also application fee, class retreats
Academic Specialty: College prep
Honors/Advanced Placement Classes: Yes
International Baccalaureate Program: No
Resources, Special Learning Needs: No
Profile: Est. 1896. Hyde Park. Grades Pre-K–12. Founded by the education
    philosopher John Dewey and based on his educational theory of com-
    plete mental, physical, and moral development of the individual.
Unique Traits: 30–35% of each year's graduating class are National Merit
    Scholarship semifinalists
Public Transportation:
        CTA Bus: 59th, Stony Island
Dress Code: Appropriate casual; jeans acceptable
Admission Requirements: Application, entrance exam, school recom-
    mendations, parent interview
Academic Scholarships: No

Public High Schools

Introduction

The Chicago Public School (CPS) system currently divides the city into six instructional areas. Students are automatically enrolled in their neighborhood school but may apply to any school in the city, provided it is not overcrowded. When searching out a public school in Chicago, pay particular attention to the different types of schools available.

Charter Schools operate independently and have their own individual missions, though they are funded by and accountable to the CPS system. Their school boards usually include representatives from community organizations, universities, foundations, and teaching staff. Charter schools have no entrance criteria and are open to all students on a lottery basis.

With no more than five hundred students, small schools provide personalized learning and individual support. They can stand on their own or share a building with another school (a school-within-a-school). Magnet schools offer challenging, subject-specific curriculum. Selective enrollment schools are challenging and competition is intense. Most classes are at the Honors and the Advanced Placement (AP) levels. These eight selective enrollment public high schools are Gwendolyn Brooks, Jones, Martin Luther King, Lane Technical, Lindblom, Northside, Walter Payton, and Whitney Young.

At most Chicago public schools, computerized lotteries ensure that all students have an equal opportunity for acceptance. There are three types of lotteries: sibling lotteries are conducted only for students who already have a brother or sister attending the school; proximity lotteries are conducted at magnet schools for students who reside within a 2.5-mile radius of the school; and general lotteries are conducted for students who are not included in either of the classifications above. Parents and guardians are welcome to observe the conducting of the lotteries.

At the selective enrollment schools, applicants must first complete an application (available in the fall at any selective enrollment school, public elementary school, or at the high school fair). Grade school achievement and "stanines" come into play here. A stanine is a national numeric standard that ranges from 1–9 to denote grade level achievement: 1–3 indicates below-average grades, 4–6 indicates average grades, and 7–9 indicates above-average grades. (Students must have a minimum stanine of 5 in both math and reading to qualify.) This application is then turned in to the student's current school. They include her 7th grade achievement test scores, 7th grade final grades, and a principal recommendation, and then forward it on. If she meets the requirements, an exam date is assigned. Admission decisions are made by each individual school and are mailed in mid-February.

When reviewing Chicago public school options, look for special designations and awards given to schools. The Prairie State Achievement Exam (PSAE) is administered to all 11th grade students and measures state learning standards.

Some Chicago public schools introduce students to a unique range of academic programs. The Greek philosopher, Socrates, inspired the Colloquium and Paideia Programs. Metropolitan Studies focuses on urban resources, and students leave the Scholars Program with dual high school and college credits.

For the student who has already narrowed down his options, many public schools in Chicago offer a variety of career-focused programs. Students may either combine academic or vocational training with their specific course of study for a college or a career preparatory (prep) program. Whether the CISCO computer program, the Junior Reserve Officer Training Corps (JROTC), or a specific career academy, most programs are enhanced by local business or even corporate sponsors who provide mentoring and work experience, which could lead to possible paid internships, college credit or industry certification. Refer to the Resource Guide for further information on all of these special programs.

A good way to put all your information into perspective is to attend the annual Chicago Public Schools' High School Fair in early fall at McCormick Place. Each year, over 45,000 students and their parents visit booths, meet educators and students, and gather information. Admission is free. For more information, call the Office of High School Programs at (773) 553-3540.

Public High Schools: Coed

Public High Schools: Girls

Academy of Applied Arts, Science & Technology High School

730 North Pulaski Road Chicago, IL 60624
Phone Number: (773) 534-6500
Fax Number: (773) 534-6504

Web Site: www.cps.k12.il.us
E-mail: See Web site
Principal: Ms. Carole Collins Ayanlaja
Admissions Contact: Ms. Carole Collins Ayanlaja
Gender: Coed

Total Enrollment: 350–400   *Student to Faculty Ratio:* 12:1
Number of Freshmen: 140   *Percentage of College Bound Grads:* 70%
Average Class Size: 23   *Tuition:* N/A

Other Expenditures: N/A
Academic Specialty: College and career prep
Honors/Advanced Placement Classes: Yes
International Baccalaureate Program: No
Resources, Special Learning Needs: No
Profile: Est. 2004. West side. Small school located in the former Orr High
   School. Rigorous curriculum. Technical career programs.
Unique Traits: Thematic course of study
Public Transportation:
   CTA L: Blue Line Pulaski, Red Line Chicago
   CTA Bus: Chicago, Pulaski
Dress Code: Appropriate casual; jeans acceptable, school polo shirt
Admission Requirements: Priority given to students living in attendance
   area; random lottery
Academic Scholarships: N/A

Academy of Communications and Technology Charter High School

4319 West Washington Boulevard Chicago, IL 60624
Phone Number: (773) 626-4200
Fax Number: (773) 626-4268

Web Site: www.cps.k12.il.us
E-mail: See Web site
Principal: Ms. Sarah Howard
Admissions Contact: Ms. Kavie Barnes
Gender: Coed

Total Enrollment: 320	*Student to Faculty Ratio:* 13:1
Number of Freshmen: 50	*Percentage of College Bound Grads:* 80%
Average Class Size: 20–25	*Tuition:* N/A

Other Expenditures: N/A
Academic Specialty: College prep
Honors/Advanced Placement Classes: No
International Baccalaureate Program: No
Resources, Special Learning Needs: Yes
Profile: Est. 1997. West Garfield Park. Grades 6–12. Cross-curriculum programs in communications, arts, and technology. Mandatory field experience.
Unique Traits: Graduation by portfolio
Public Transportation:
     CTA L: Green Line Pulaski
     CTA Bus: Madison
Dress Code: Khaki slacks, school shirt, dress shoes
Admission Requirements: Accepts students citywide; random lottery
Academic Scholarships: N/A

Amundsen High School

5110 North Damen Avenue Chicago, IL 60625
Phone Number: (773) 534-2320
Fax Number: (773) 534-2330

Web Site: www.amundsen.cps.k12.il.us
E-mail: See Web site
Principal: Mr. Carlos Munoz, Acting Principal
Admissions Contact: Ms. Jessica Connolly
Gender: Coed

Total Enrollment: 1,550   *Student to Faculty Ratio:* 18:1
Number of Freshmen: 470   *Percentage of College Bound Grads:* 75%
Average Class Size: 25–28   *Tuition:* N/A

Other Expenditures: N/A
Academic Specialty: College prep
Honors/Advanced Placement Classes: Yes
International Baccalaureate Program: Yes
Resources, Special Learning Needs: Yes
Profile: Est. 1929. Ravenswood. School-within-a-school. Ethnically diverse. Bilingual student body. Small learning communities. Award-winning landscape cultivated by student body.
Unique Traits: Newly remodeled stadium
Public Transportation:
    CTA Bus: Damen, Foster
Dress Code: Navy slacks, white polo shirt
Admission Requirements: Priority given to students living in attendance area; random lottery. IB program: accepts students citywide based on academic achievement
Academic Scholarships: N/A

Architecture, Construction and Engineering (ACE) Technical High School

5410 South State Street Chicago, IL 60609
Phone Number: (773) 548-8705
Fax Number: (773) 548-8706

Web Site: www.cps.k12.il.us
E-mail: See Web site
Principal: Ms. Geri Harston, Executive Director
Admissions Contact: Mr. Daniel Kramer, Director of Education
Gender: Coed

Total Enrollment: 125–500   *Student to Faculty Ratio:* 15:1
Number of Freshmen: 140   *Percentage of College Bound Grads:* N/A
Average Class Size: 20–24   *Tuition:* N/A

Other Expenditures: N/A
Academic Specialty: Career prep
Honors/Advanced Placement Classes: No
International Baccalaureate Program: No
Resources, Special Learning Needs: Yes
Profile: Est. 2004. Washington Park. Rigorous curriculum. Vocational education programs within the construction industry (labor, management, and professional services) designed by construction industry leaders.
Unique Traits: Thematic course of study
Public Transportation:
        CTA L: Green Line State, Red Line State
        CTA Bus: State
Dress Code: Blue slacks or skirt, school polo shirt, dress shoes
Admission Requirements: Accepts students citywide; random lottery
Academic Scholarships: N/A

Big Picture Company High School at Back of the Yards

4946 South Paulina Street Chicago, IL 60609
Phone Number: (773) 535-9219
Fax Number: (773) 535-9477

Web Site: www.bigpicture.org
E-mail: See Web site
Principal: Mr. Alfred Nambo
Admissions Contact: Mr. Alfred Nambo
Gender: Coed

Total Enrollment: 60–120   *Student to Faculty Ratio:* 15:1
Number of Freshmen: 30   *Percentage of College Bound Grads:* N/A
Average Class Size: 15   *Tuition:* N/A

Other Expenditures: N/A
Academic Specialty: College prep
Honors/Advanced Placement Classes: Yes
International Baccalaureate Program: No
Resources, Special Learning Needs: Yes
Profile: Est. 2003. South side. Small school located in the Cesar Chavez MultiCultural High School. Traditional classes are replaced by the student's individual learning plan, which is guided by a teacher, parent, and mentor.
Unique Traits: Operated by the Big Picture Company, a not-for-profit organization dedicated to new schooling concepts
Public Transportation:
    CTA Bus: Ashland, 51st
Dress Code: Appropriate casual; jeans acceptable
Admission Requirements: Priority given to students living in attendance area; random lottery
Academic Scholarships: N/A

Big Picture Company High School at Williams

2710 South Dearborn Street Chicago, IL 60620
Phone Number: (773) 534-9160
Fax Number: (773) 534-9223

Web Site: www.bigpicture.org
E-mail: See Web site
Principal: Ms. Kothyn Alexander
Admissions Contact: Ms. Loretta Evans
Gender: Coed

Total Enrollment: 60–120   *Student to Faculty Ratio:* 15:1
Number of Freshmen: 30   *Percentage of College Bound Grads:* N/A
Average Class Size: 15   *Tuition:* N/A

Other Expenditures: N/A
Academic Specialty: College prep
Honors/Advanced Placement Classes: Yes
International Baccalaureate Program: No
Resources, Special Learning Needs: Yes
Profile: Est. 2003. Bronzeville. Small school. Traditional classes are replaced by the student's individual learning plan, which is guided by a teacher, parent, and mentor.
Unique Traits: Operated by the Big Picture Company, a not-for-profit organization dedicated to new schooling concepts
Public Transportation:
    CTA L: Red Line 35th
    CTA Bus: State
Dress Code: Appropriate casual; jeans acceptable
Admission Requirements: Priority given to students living in attendance area; random lottery
Academic Scholarships: N/A

William J. Bogan Computer Technical High School

3939 West 79th Street Chicago, IL 60652
Phone Number: (773) 535-2180
Fax Number: (773) 535-2165

Web Site: www.bogan.cps.k12.il.us
E-mail: See Web site
Principal: Mr. Robert C. Miller
Admissions Contact: Ms. Merry M. Watson
Gender: Coed

Total Enrollment: 2,095   *Student to Faculty Ratio:* 28:1
Number of Freshmen: 627   *Percentage of College Bound Grads:* 45%
Average Class Size: 29   *Tuition:* N/A

Other Expenditures: N/A
Academic Specialty: College and career prep
Honors/Advanced Placement Classes: Yes
International Baccalaureate Program: Yes
Resources, Special Learning Needs: Yes
Profile: Est. 1958. Southwest. Specializing in computer technology studies and the use of technology throughout the curriculum. Career Academies. Education-to-Careers programs.
Unique Traits: Named one of the "Top Wired Schools" in *Family PC* magazine
Public Transportation:
       CTA L: Orange Line Pulaski
Dress Code: Black slacks, white shirt, black shoes
Admission Requirements: Priority given to students living in attendance area; random lottery. IB program: acceptance based on academic achievement
Academic Scholarships: N/A

Bowen Environmental Studies Team (BEST) High School

2710 East 89th Street Chicago, IL 60617
Phone Number: (773) 535-6597
Fax Number: (773) 535-6598

Web Site: www.best.cps.k12.il.us
E-mail: See Web site
Principal: Dr. JoAnn Thomas-Woods
Admissions Contact: Ms. Gloria Gomez
Gender: Coed

Total Enrollment: 320–500   *Student to Faculty Ratio:* 10:1
Number of Freshmen: 100   *Percentage of College Bound Grads:* N/A
Average Class Size: 20   *Tuition:* N/A

Other Expenditures: N/A
Academic Specialty: College and career prep
Honors/Advanced Placement Classes: Yes
International Baccalaureate Program: No
Resources, Special Learning Needs: Yes
Profile: Est. 2002. Southeast. Small school located in the Bowen campus. Focus on the environment (redeveloping urban environments and nearby wetlands). Partnerships with local, city, and state agencies and organizations. Classroom and service learning. Education-to-Careers programs.
Unique Traits: Thematic course of study
Public Transportation:
>   CTA L: Red Line 87th
>   CTA Bus: South Chicago
Dress Code: Dark slacks or skirt, school polo shirt
Admission Requirements: Priority is given to students living in attendance area; random lottery.
Academic Scholarships: N/A

Gwendolyn Brooks College Preparatory Academy

250 East 111th Street Chicago, IL 60628
Phone Number: (773) 535-9930
Fax Number: (773) 535-9939

Web Site: www.brooks.cps.k12.il.us
E-mail: See Web site
Principal: Dr. Pamela G. Dyson
Admissions Contact: Mr. Robert Kobylski
Gender: Coed

Total Enrollment: 800   *Student to Faculty Ratio:* 15:1
Number of Freshmen: 175   *Percentage of College Bound Grads:* 85%
Average Class Size: 28   *Tuition:* N/A

Other Expenditures: N/A
Academic Specialty: College prep
Honors/Advanced Placement Classes: Yes
International Baccalaureate Program: Yes
Resources, Special Learning Needs: Yes
Profile: Est. 1998. Pullman. Selective Enrollment School. 40-acre campus. Rigorous academic program; all classes are at an honors+ level. Personalized student academic plans. School divided into a junior and senior academy. Corporate and college partnerships.
Unique Traits: Only 10% of prospective students are accepted
Public Transportation:
     CTA Bus: King
Dress Code: Blue slacks or skirt, white polo shirt
Admission Requirements: Accepts freshmen students citywide; entrance exam, transcripts
Academic Scholarships: N/A

George Washington Carver Military Academy

13100 South Doty Avenue Chicago, IL 60827
Phone Number: (773) 535-5250
Fax Number: (773) 535-5037

Web Site: www.carvermilitary.cps.k12.il.us
E-mail: See web site
Principal: Mr. William Johnson, EdD
Admissions Contact: Ms. Kathryn Alderson
Gender: Coed

Total Enrollment: 800   *Student to Faculty Ratio:* 14:1
Number of Freshmen: 250   *Percentage of College Bound Grads:* 65%
Average Class Size: 28   *Tuition:* N/A

Other Expenditures: N/A
Academic Specialty: College and career prep
Honors/Advanced Placement Classes: Yes
International Baccalaureate Program: No
Resources, Special Learning Needs: Yes
Profile: Est. 1999. Southeast side. Military leadership program combined
   with either an Education-to-Careers or college prep program. After
   the first year, students choose their area of concentration. JROTC.
Unique Traits: The largest high school military academy in the U.S.
Public Transportation:
   CTA Bus: 130th
Dress Code: Standard government military uniform
Admission Requirements: Accepts freshmen students citywide; transcripts,
   interview, recommendations
Academic Scholarships: N/A

Chicago Academy High School

3400 North Austin Avenue Chicago, IL 60634
Phone Number: (773) 534-0146
Fax Number: (773) 534-0192

Web Site: www.chicagoacademy.org/highschool
E-mail: ttsmith@cps.k12.il.us
Principal: Mr. Brian Sims
Admissions Contact: Ms. Terika Smith
Gender: Coed

Total Enrollment: 250–500   *Student to Faculty Ratio:* 10:1
Number of Freshmen: 125   *Percentage of College Bound Grads:* N/A
Average Class Size: 25   *Tuition:* N/A

Other Expenditures: N/A
Academic Specialty: College prep
Honors/Advanced Placement Classes: No
International Baccalaureate Program: No
Resources, Special Learning Needs: Yes
Profile: Est. 2004. Portage Park. Small school. Extended classes for hands-on learning. Focusing on community building, skill development, and academic support.
Unique Traits: Small learning communities for a diverse group of academic levels
Public Transportation:
   CTA Bus: Austin, Belmont, Addison
Dress Code: Appropriate casual; jeans acceptable
Admission Requirements: Accepts students citywide
Academic Scholarships: N/A

Chicago Discovery Academy

2710 East 89th Street Chicago, IL 60617
Phone Number: (773) 535-7947
Fax Number: (773) 535-6930

Web Site: www.cps.k12.il.us
E-mail: See web site
Principal: Ms. Lynne Nuzzo
Admissions Contact: Ms. Judith Wiatrowski
Gender: Coed

Total Enrollment: 400   *Student to Faculty Ratio:* 13:1
Number of Freshmen: 140   *Percentage of College Bound Grads:* 95%
Average Class Size: 28   *Tuition:* N/A

Other Expenditures: N/A
Academic Specialty: College prep
Honors/Advanced Placement Classes: Yes
International Baccalaureate Program: No
Resources, Special Learning Needs: Yes
Profile: Est. 2003. Southeast side. Small school located in Bowen Campus.
    Challenging academics. Specializing in architecture, art, and college
    prep. Education-to-Careers programs. JROTC.
Unique Traits: Field trips developed through city institution partnerships
Public Transportation:
    CTA L: Red Line 87th
    CTA Bus: South Chicago
Dress Code: Blue or black slacks or skirt, school polo shirt
Admission Requirements: Priority given to students living in attendance
    area; random lottery
Academic Scholarships: N/A

Chicago High School for Agricultural Sciences

3857 West 111th Street Chicago, IL 60655
Phone Number: (773) 535-2500
Fax Number: (773) 535-2507

Web Site: www.chicagoagr.cps.k12.il.us
E-mail: mhamilton@cps.k12.il.us
Principal: Mr. David Gilligan
Admissions Contact: Ms. Martha Hamilton
Gender: Coed

Total Enrollment: 600	*Student to Faculty Ratio:* 12:1
Number of Freshmen: 150	*Percentage of College Bound Grads:* 80%
Average Class Size: 28	*Tuition:* N/A

Other Expenditures: N/A
Academic Specialty: College prep
Honors/Advanced Placement Classes: Yes
International Baccalaureate Program: No
Resources, Special Learning Needs: Yes
Profile: Est. 1985. Mount Greenwood. Magnet School. Agricultural science and business. 72-acre land lab located on the last existing farm in Chicago. Innovative hands-on curriculum for talented science and math students. Named a "New American School" by the U.S. Department of Education. Summer employment and internship programs at the University of Illinois and Michigan State.
Unique Traits: Only school of its kind in the Midwest. Serves as a model for other like schools across the country.
Public Transportation:
  CTA Bus: Pulaski, 111th
Dress Code: Appropriate casual; jeans acceptable
Admission Requirements: Accepts students citywide; minimum stanine of 5 in reading and math, lottery
Academic Scholarships: N/A

Chicago International Charter
High School—Longwood

1309 West 95th Street Chicago, IL 60643
Phone Number: (773) 238-5330
Fax Number: (773) 238-5350

Web Site: www.cps.k12.il.us
E-mail: See Web site
Principal: Mr. Robert Lang
Admissions Contact: Charter School Foundation: (312) 455-7890
Gender: Coed

Total Enrollment: 1,350   *Student to Faculty Ratio:* 20:1
Number of Freshmen: 95   *Percentage of College Bound Grads:* 90%
Average Class Size: 25   *Tuition:* N/A

Other Expenditures: N/A
Academic Specialty: College prep
Honors/Advanced Placement Classes: No
International Baccalaureate Program: No
Resources, Special Learning Needs: Yes
Profile: Est. 1997. South side. Grades K–12. Based on the Edison School
     curriculum: individual attention and mentoring, longer school day and
     year. Students in grades 3–12 are given a computer for home use.
Unique Traits: Unique curriculum
Public Transportation:
     CTA L: Red Line 95th
Dress Code: Gray or blue slacks or skirt, maroon shirt, tie for boys
Admission Requirements: Accepts students citywide; random lottery
Academic Scholarships: N/A

Chicago International Charter High School— Northtown Academy

3900 West Peterson Avenue Chicago, IL 60659
Phone Number: (773) 478-3655
Fax Number: (773) 478-6029

Web Site: www.cicsnorthtown.org
E-mail: See Web site
Principal: Ms. Loren Fields, Director
Admissions Contact: Ms. Laura Smith
Gender: Coed

Total Enrollment: 550	*Student to Faculty Ratio:* 13:1
Number of Freshmen: 180	*Percentage of College Bound Grads:* 95%
Average Class Size: 23	*Tuition:* N/A

Other Expenditures: N/A
Academic Specialty: College prep
Honors/Advanced Placement Classes: Yes
International Baccalaureate Program: No
Resources, Special Learning Needs: Yes
Profile: Est. 2003. Peterson Park. Charter school. Rigorous academic program. Small size. 4-year advisory program.
Unique Traits: Focused on advanced instruction
Public Transportation:
    CTA Bus: Peterson, Pulaski
Dress Code: Gray or blue slacks, white shirt, blue sweater, ties for boys
Admission Requirements: Accepts students citywide; random lottery
Academic Scholarships: N/A

Chicago Mathematics and Science Academy Charter School

1709 West Lunt Avenue Chicago, IL 60626
Phone Number: (773) 761-8960
Fax Number: (773) 761-8961

Web Site: www.cmsaonline.net
E-mail: See Web site
Principal: Mr. Salim Ucan, Executive Director
Admissions Contact: Mr. Salim Ucan
Gender: Coed

Total Enrollment: 225–525   *Student to Faculty Ratio:* 16:1
Number of Freshmen: 75   *Percentage of College Bound Grads:* N/A
Average Class Size: 25   *Tuition:* N/A

Other Expenditures: N/A
Academic Specialty: College prep
Honors/Advanced Placement Classes: Yes
International Baccalaureate Program: No
Resources, Special Learning Needs: Yes
Profile: Est. 2004. Rogers Park. Grades 6–12. Rigorous academic program focusing on math, science, and technology. Extended school hours and year. High level of parent involvement. Local, national, and international field trips.
Unique Traits: Part of 8 concept schools, a nonprofit educational management organization
Public Transportation:
     CTA L: Red Line Morse
     CTA Bus: Lunt
Dress Code: Navy or khaki slacks, blue or maroon school shirt
Admission Requirements: Accepts students citywide; random lottery
Academic Scholarships: N/A

Chicago Military Academy—Bronzeville

3519 South Giles Street Chicago, IL 60653
Phone Number: (773) 534-9750
Fax Number: (773) 534-9768

Web Site: www.chicagomilitary.cps.k12.il.us
E-mail: See Web site
Principal: Mr. Richard Gray
Admissions Contact: Ms. Jeanette Howard
Gender: Coed

Total Enrollment: 500   *Student to Faculty Ratio:* 24:1
Number of Freshmen: 140   *Percentage of College Bound Grads:* 85%
Average Class Size: 25   *Tuition:* N/A

Other Expenditures: N/A
Academic Specialty: College prep
Honors/Advanced Placement Classes: Yes
International Baccalaureate Program: No
Resources, Special Learning Needs: Yes
Profile: Est. 1999. Bronzeville. Military leadership; mandatory JROTC
  program (Army). Curriculum stresses language arts, math, science,
  and technology. Education-to-Careers programs.
Unique Traits: The city's first comprehensive military academy for high
  school students
Public Transportation:
  CTA L: Green Line 35th
Dress Code: Government standard military uniform
Admission Requirements: Accepts freshmen students citywide; academic
  achievement, interview, recommendation
Academic Scholarships: N/A

Chicago Vocational Career Academy

2100 East 87th Street Chicago, IL 66017
Phone Number: (773) 535-6099
Fax Number: (773) 535-6633

Web Site: www.cvca.cps.k12.il.us
E-mail: See Web site
Principal: Ms. Marie Chambers-Miles
Admissions Contact: Ms. Shirley Carter
Gender: Coed

Total Enrollment: 2,000   *Student to Faculty Ratio:* 20:1
Number of Freshmen: 600   *Percentage of College Bound Grads:* 65%
Average Class Size: 25   *Tuition:* N/A

Other Expenditures: N/A
Academic Specialty: College and career prep
Honors/Advanced Placement Classes: Yes
International Baccalaureate Program: No
Resources, Special Learning Needs: Yes
Profile: Est. 1942. Southeast side. State-of-the-art technology labs. Student owned and operated businesses. Internships and apprenticeships. On-the-job training and part-time employment. Education-to-Careers programs. JROTC. Accelerated training and certification programs.
Unique Traits: More Education-to-Careers programs than any other Chicago public school. The Diesel Technology program is ranked first in the city.
Public Transportation:
    CTA Bus: 87th, Jeffrey
Dress Code: Blue slacks, skirt, or skort; white, navy, or gold school polo shirt
Admission Requirements: Accepts students citywide with a 5+ stanine
Academic Scholarships: N/A

Michele Clark Academic Preparatory High School

5101 West Harrison Street Chicago, IL 60644
Phone Number: (773) 534-6250
Fax Number: (773) 534-6292

Web Site: www.micheleclark.org
E-mail: See Web site
Principal: Ms. Annette Gurley
Admissions Contact: Ms. Debra Thomas, Ms. Rosalind Taylor
Gender: Coed

Total Enrollment: 818
Number of Freshmen: 228
Average Class Size: 20–25

Student to Faculty Ratio: 12:1
Percentage of College Bound Grads: N/A
Tuition: N/A

Other Expenditures: N/A
Academic Specialty: College prep
Honors/Advanced Placement Classes: Yes
International Baccalaureate Program: Yes
Resources, Special Learning Needs: Yes
Profile: Est. 2002. South Austin. Grades 6–12. Magnet school. IB Program
    for grades 6–10
Unique Traits: Named a CPS "Rising Star"
Public Transportation:
    CTA L: Green Line Laramie, Blue Line Cicero
    CTA Bus: Harrison
Dress Code: Appropriate casual; jeans acceptable
Admission Requirements: Accepts students citywide. IB program: required
    stanine of 6 in reading and math
Academic Scholarships: N/A

Roberto Clemente Community Academy High School

1147 North Western Avenue Chicago, IL 60622
Phone Number: (773) 534-4000
Fax Number: (773) 534-4012

Web Site: www.clementehs.org
E-mail: See Web site
Principal: Ms. Irene M. DaMota
Admissions Contact: Mr. Renee Ortman
Gender: Coed

Total Enrollment: 2,100   *Student to Faculty Ratio:* 17:1
Number of Freshmen: 650   *Percentage of College Bound Grads:* 60%
Average Class Size: 28   *Tuition:* N/A

Other Expenditures: N/A
Academic Specialty: College and career prep
Honors/Advanced Placement Classes: Yes
International Baccalaureate Program: No
Resources, Special Learning Needs: Yes
Profile: Est. 1974. Northwest side. 6 small schools-within-a-school. Education-to-Careers programs.
Unique Traits: Award winning culinary arts program
Public Transportation:
          CTA Bus: Division, Western
Dress Code: Blue or black slacks, white polo shirt
Admission Requirements: Priority given to students living in attendance area; random lottery. Math, Science, and Technology Academy: accepts freshmen students citywide
Academic Scholarships: N/A

George Washington Collins High School

1313 South Sacramento Drive Chicago, IL 60623
Phone Number: (773) 534-1500
Fax Number: (773) 534-1399

Web Site: www.cps.k12.il.us
E-mail: See Web site
Principal: Mr. Andrew Denton, III
Admissions Contact: Ms. Sheila Banks
Gender: Coed

Total Enrollment: 844   *Student to Faculty Ratio:* 17:1
Number of Freshmen: 316   *Percentage of College Bound Grads:* 75%
Average Class Size: 26   *Tuition:* N/A

Other Expenditures: Activity fee
Academic Specialty: College prep
Honors/Advanced Placement Classes: Yes
International Baccalaureate Program: No
Resources, Special Learning Needs: Yes
Profile: Est. 1975. West side. Technology-rich environment: 4 computer
   labs, mobile lab, wireless internet. JROTC won 3rd place in citywide
   competition. Allied Health programs partnership with area hospitals.
   Student internships.
Unique Traits: Academic Decathlon team has won 29 medals
Public Transportation:
   CTA L: Blue Line Kedzie
   CTA Bus: Roosevelt, Kedzie
Dress Code: Khaki slacks or skirt, white polo shirt
Admission Requirements: Priority given to students living in attendance
   area
Academic Scholarships: N/A

Community Links High School

2400 South Marshall Boulevard Chicago, IL 60623
Phone Number: (773) 534-1997
Fax Number: (773) 534-0354

Web Site: www.cps.k12.il.us
E-mail: See Web site
Principal: Dr. Carlos Azcoitia
Admissions Contact: Mr. Sergio Almazan
Gender: Coed

Total Enrollment: 93–100   *Student to Faculty Ratio:* 16:1
Number of Freshmen: 32   *Percentage of College Bound Grads:* N/A
Average Class Size: 17   *Tuition:* N/A

Other Expenditures: N/A
Academic Specialty: College prep
Honors/Advanced Placement Classes: Yes
International Baccalaureate Program: No
Resources, Special Learning Needs: Yes
Profile: Est. 2003. Little Village. Small school located in the John Spry
   Elementary School. Focus is on rigorous academics and community
   service. Students work as tutors and teaching assistants at elementary
   school. Mandatory JROTC/Physical Education program fosters disci-
   pline and teamwork.
Unique Traits: A year-round 3-year program; students graduate early
Public Transportation:
   CTA L: Blue Line California
   CTA Bus: California
Dress Code: Navy or black slacks, solid color polo shirt or blouse
Admission Requirements: Preference given to students living in attendance
   area and/or Spry Elementary grads; interview, random lottery
Academic Scholarships: N/A

George H. Corliss High School

821 East 103rd Street Chicago, IL 60628
Phone Number: (773) 535-5115
Fax Number: (773) 535-5511

Web Site: www.corliss.cps.k12.il.us
E-mail: See Web site
Principal: Dr. Anthony Spivey
Admissions Contact: Ms. Erica Dice
Gender: Coed

Total Enrollment: 1,000   *Student to Faculty Ratio:* 17:1
Number of Freshmen: 325   *Percentage of College Bound Grads:* 50%
Average Class Size: 28   *Tuition:* N/A

Other Expenditures: N/A
Academic Specialty: College prep
Honors/Advanced Placement Classes: Yes
International Baccalaureate Program: No
Resources, Special Learning Needs: Yes
Profile: Est. 1974. Pullman. Small school. Schools-within-a-school. School
   of Navy Science and Technology (JROTC). School of Finance. Fast
   Trek (students graduate with college credits). Education-to-Careers
   programs. Fine and Performing Arts Magnet program.
Unique Traits: Program variety
Public Transportation:
   CTA Bus: 106th, 108th
Dress Code: Black slacks or skirt, white polo shirt
Admission Requirements: Priority given to students living in attendance
   area
Academic Scholarships: N/A

Richard T. Crane Technical Preparatory Common School

2245 West Jackson Boulevard Chicago, IL 60612
Phone Number: (773) 534-7550
Fax Number: (773) 534-7557

Web Site: www.crane.cps.k12.il.us
E-mail: See Web site
Principal: Mr. Melver L. Scott
Admissions Contact: Ms. Loretta Lesley
Gender: Coed

Total Enrollment: 1,300	*Student to Faculty Ratio:* 16:1
Number of Freshmen: 400	*Percentage of College Bound Grads:* 75%
Average Class Size: 28	*Tuition:* N/A

Other Expenditures: N/A
Academic Specialty: College and career prep
Honors/Advanced Placement Classes: Yes
International Baccalaureate Program: No
Resources, Special Learning Needs: Yes
Profile: Est. 1970. West side. Schools-within-a-school. Math, Science, and Technology Academy. Education-to-Careers programs. Technology Academy.
Unique Traits: A 52-station technology lab
Public Transportation:
　　CTA L: Blue Line Western
　　CTA Bus: Jackson
Dress Code: Appropriate casual; jeans acceptable
Admission Requirements: Priority given to students living in attendance area. Academies accept students citywide
Academic Scholarships: N/A

Curie Metropolitan High School

4959 South Archer Avenue Chicago, IL 60632
Phone Number: (773) 535-2100
Fax Number: (773) 535-4900

Web Site: www.curiehs.org
E-mail: See Web site
Principal: Ms. Jerrelyn Jones
Admissions Contact: Ms. Ana Espinoza
Gender: Coed

Total Enrollment: 3,000   *Student to Faculty Ratio:* 14:1
Number of Freshmen: 850   *Percentage of College Bound Grads:* 45%
Average Class Size: 28   *Tuition:* N/A

Other Expenditures: N/A
Academic Specialty: College and career prep
Honors/Advanced Placement Classes: Yes
International Baccalaureate Program: Yes
Resources, Special Learning Needs: Yes
Profile: Est. 1973. Archer Heights. Magnet School. Rare offering of three
magnet programs: IB, fine arts, and vocational. Education-to-Careers
programs.
Unique Traits: Named the Best Art Program in the State by the Illinois Art
Education Association
Public Transportation:
    CTA L: Orange Line Archer, Pulaski
Dress Code: Appropriate casual; jeans acceptable
Admission Requirements: Accepts freshmen students citywide;
5+ stanine.
Academic Scholarships: N/A

Paul L. Dunbar Vocational Career Academy

3000 South King Drive Chicago, IL 60616
Phone Number: (773) 534-9000
Fax Number: (773) 534-9250

Web Site: www.dunbar.cps.k12.il.us
E-mail: See Web site
Principal: Dr. Barbara A. Hall
Admissions Contact: Ms. Linda Valentine
Gender: Coed

Total Enrollment: 1,650	*Student to Faculty Ratio:* 23:1
Number of Freshmen: 500	*Percentage of College Bound Grads:* 60%
Average Class Size: 28	*Tuition:* N/A

Other Expenditures: N/A
Academic Specialty: Career prep
Honors/Advanced Placement Classes: Yes
International Baccalaureate Program: No
Resources, Special Learning Needs: Yes
Profile: Est. 1942. Bronzeville. Trade school. 12-acre lakefront campus. Seventeen vocational shops. Medial and resource center. 4 science labs. Tutorial, journalism, and distance learning labs. Education-to-Careers programs.
Unique Traits: An award winning trade school
Public Transportation:
  CTA L: Red Line 35th
  CTA Bus: State
Dress Code: Appropriate casual; no jeans
Admission Requirements: Accepts students citywide; stanine of 5+, random lottery
Academic Scholarships: N/A

DuSable Multiplex Campus

4934 South Wabash Avenue Chicago, IL 60615
Phone Number: (773) 535-1100
Fax Number: (773) 535-1004

Web Site: www.cps.k12.il.us
E-mail: See Web site
Principal: Ms. Linda Layne, Campus Manager
Admissions Contact: Ms. Linda Layne
Gender: Coed

Total Enrollment: 125–500   *Student to Faculty Ratio:* N/A
Number of Freshmen: 125   *Percentage of College Bound Grads:* N/A
Average Class Size: N/A   *Tuition:* N/A

Other Expenditures: N/A
Academic Specialty: College prep
Honors/Advanced Placement Classes: Yes
International Baccalaureate Program: Yes
Resources, Special Learning Needs: Yes
Profile: Est. 2005. Bronzeville. 4 small schools on one campus. Specializing in careers not historically minority representative: medicine, forensic science, investment banking, and mortuary science.
Unique Traits: A small school campus
Public Transportation:
      CTA Bus: State
Dress Code: Appropriate casual; no jeans
Admission Requirements: Priority given to students living in attendance area
Academic Scholarships: N/A

Walter H. Dyett Academic Center

555 East 51st Street Chicago, IL 60615
Phone Number: (773) 535-1825
Fax Number: (773) 535-1037

Web Site: www.dyett.cps.k12.il.us
E-mail: See Web site
Principal: Ms. Cheryl Marshall-Washington
Admissions Contact: Ms. Ruth Jordan
Gender: Coed

Total Enrollment: 515   *Student to Faculty Ratio:* 14:1
Number of Freshmen: 140   *Percentage of College Bound Grads:* 15%
Average Class Size: 25–32   *Tuition:* N/A

Other Expenditures: N/A
Academic Specialty: College and career prep
Honors/Advanced Placement Classes: Yes
International Baccalaureate Program: No
Resources, Special Learning Needs: Yes
Profile: Est. 1999. Washington Park. Grades 7–12. Strong technology curriculum. Commitment to discipline. Education-to-Careers programs.
Unique Traits: In-school bank operated by students
Public Transportation:
       CTA *Bus:* 51st, King
Dress Code: Black slacks or skirt, white shirt or blouse, tie for boys
Admission Requirements: Priority given to students living in attendance area
Academic Scholarships: N/A

Englewood Technical Preparatory Academy

6201 South Stewart Avenue Chicago, IL 60621
Phone Number: (773) 535-3600
Fax Number: (773) 535-3586

Web Site: www.englewood.cps.k12.il.us
E-mail: See Web site
Principal: Ms. Diane L. Jackson
Admissions Contact: Mr. Bennie Hamilton
Gender: Coed

Total Enrollment: 858	*Student to Faculty Ratio:* 13:1
Number of Freshmen: 126	*Percentage of College Bound Grads:* 25%
Average Class Size: 25	*Tuition:* N/A

Other Expenditures: N/A
Academic Specialty: College and career prep
Honors/Advanced Placement Classes: Yes
International Baccalaureate Program: No
Resources, Special Learning Needs: Yes
Profile: Est. 1898. Englewood. Known as a premier school in its area. Education-to-Careers programs. JROTC has won multiple local and state awards.
Unique Traits: Named a CPS "Rising Star" high school
Public Transportation:
    CTA L: Green Line 63rd
Dress Code: Appropriate casual; no jeans
Admission Requirements: Priority given to student living in attendance area
Academic Scholarships: N/A

Excel Academy

730 North Pulaski Road Chicago, IL 60624
Phone Number: (773) 534-6500
Fax Number: (773) 534-6504

Web Site: www.cps.k12.il.us
E-mail: See Web site
Principal: Ms. Marva Whaley-Anoban
Admissions Contact: Ms. Marva Whaley-Anoban
Gender: Coed

Total Enrollment: 500   *Student to Faculty Ratio:* 10:1
Number of Freshmen: 150   *Percentage of College Bound Grads:* 50%
Average Class Size: 18   *Tuition:* N/A

Other Expenditures: N/A
Academic Specialty: College prep
Honors/Advanced Placement Classes: Yes
International Baccalaureate Program: No
Resources, Special Learning Needs: Yes
Profile: Est. 2004. West Garfield Park. Small school located in the former
    Orr High School. EXCEL = Educating Exceptional Children at Every
    Level. Students work as teaching assistants, interns, tutors, and job
    shadow in preparation for a teaching career.
Unique Traits: Thematic course of study
Public Transportation:
        CTA L: Green Line Pulaski
        CTA Bus: Chicago, Pulaski
Dress Code: Dark slacks, school polo shirt
Admission Requirements: Priority given to students living in attendance
    area
Academic Scholarships: N/A

David Glasgow Farragut Career Academy

2345 South Christiana Avenue Chicago, IL 60623
Phone Number: (773) 534-1300
Fax Number: (773) 534-1336

Web Site: www.farragutca.com
E-mail: See Web site
Principal: Mr. Edward Guerra
Admissions Contact: Ms. Latoya Hooker
Gender: Coed

Total Enrollment: 2500	*Student to Faculty Ratio:* 22:1
Number of Freshmen: 500	*Percentage of College Bound Grads:* 35%
Average Class Size: 28	*Tuition:* N/A

Other Expenditures: N/A
Academic Specialty: College and career prep
Honors/Advanced Placement Classes: Yes
International Baccalaureate Program: No
Resources, Special Learning Needs: Yes
Profile: Est. 1894. Little Village. Combines academics with work-study through business and community partnerships. Education-to-Careers programs. JROTC.
Unique Traits: Student-designed community law and health services clinics on site
Public Transportation:
　　CTA L: Red Line Kedzie
　　CTA Bus: Kedzie
Dress Code: Black slacks or skirt, white polo shirt
Admission Requirements: Priority given to students living in attendance area
Academic Scholarships: N/A

Christian Fenger Academy High School

11220 South Wallace Street Chicago, IL 60628
Phone Number: (773) 535-5430
Fax Number: (773) 535-5450

Web Site: www.cps.k12.il.us
E-mail: Fengerhighschool@cps.k12.il.us
Principal: Dr. William Johnson, EdD
Admissions Contact: Mr. Gerald Arena
Gender: Coed

Total Enrollment: 1,352   *Student to Faculty Ratio:* 24:1
Number of Freshmen: 356   *Percentage of College Bound Grads:* 70%
Average Class Size: 28   *Tuition:* N/A

Other Expenditures: Activity fee
Academic Specialty: College and career prep
Honors/Advanced Placement Classes: Yes
International Baccalaureate Program: No
Resources, Special Learning Needs: Yes
Profile: Est. 1926. South side. Science, Engineering, Math, and Aerospace
   Academy funded by NASA. Technology Academy. JROTC. Education-
   to-Careers programs. AVID program (rigorous curriculum for B and
   C students).
Unique Traits: Numerous special education programs
Public Transportation:
      CTA Bus: Halsted, 111th, 115th
Dress Code: Khaki slacks, red polo shirt
Admission Requirements: Priority given to students living in attendance
   area
Academic Scholarships: N/A

Edwin G. Foreman High School

3235 North LeClaire Avenue Chicago, IL 60641
Phone Number: (773) 534-3400
Fax Number: (773) 534-3684

Web Site: www.foreman.cps.k12.il.us
E-mail: See Web site
Principal: Mr. Frank Candioto
Admissions Contact: Ms. Lydia Maldonado
Gender: Coed

Total Enrollment: 1,600   *Student to Faculty Ratio:* 17:1
Number of Freshmen: 500   *Percentage of College Bound Grads:* 40%
Average Class Size: 28   *Tuition:* N/A

Other Expenditures: N/A
Academic Specialty: College and career prep
Honors/Advanced Placement Classes: Yes
International Baccalaureate Program: No
Resources, Special Learning Needs: Yes
Profile: Est. 1993. Northwest side. College-level class option. Students recruited for federally funded Upward Bound program sponsored by Columbia College and area businesses. Education-to-Careers programs. JROTC.
Unique Traits: Won first place in Coca-Cola Black History Essay Contest
Public Transportation:
        CTA Bus: Belmont
Dress Code: Black, blue, or khaki slacks or skirt; white polo shirt
Admission Requirements: Contact school
Academic Scholarships: N/A

Gage Park High School

5630 South Rockwell Street Chicago, IL 60629
Phone Number: (773) 535-9230
Fax Number: (773) 535-9411

Web Site: www.cps.k12.il.us
E-mail: See Web site
Principal: Mr. Wilfredo Ortiz
Admissions Contact: Mr. Luis Flores
Gender: Coed

Total Enrollment: 1,500   *Student to Faculty Ratio:* 22:1
Number of Freshmen: 600   *Percentage of College Bound Grads:* 64%
Average Class Size: 28   *Tuition:* N/A

Other Expenditures: N/A
Academic Specialty: College and career prep
Honors/Advanced Placement Classes: Yes
International Baccalaureate Program: No
Resources, Special Learning Needs: Yes
Profile: Est. 1940. Gage Park. School-within-a-school. Freshman Academy
    provides transitioning. AVID program (rigorous curriculum for B and
    C students). Education-to-Careers program. JROTC.
Unique Traits: Special assistance for struggling students
Public Transportation:
    CTA Bus: 55th
Dress Code: Black slacks or skirt, white polo shirt
Admission Requirements: Priority given to students living in attendance
    area
Academic Scholarships: N/A

Global Visions Academy

2710 East 89th Street Chicago, IL 60617
Phone Number: (773) 535-6905
Fax Number: (773) 535-6492

Web Site: www.cps.k12.il.us
E-mail: See Web site
Principal: Ms. Patricia Jones-Hight
Admissions Contact: Ms. Martha McKinley
Gender: Coed

Total Enrollment: 300–500   *Student to Faculty Ratio:* 15:1
Number of Freshmen: 130   *Percentage of College Bound Grads:* N/A
Average Class Size: 25   *Tuition:* N/A

Other Expenditures: N/A
Academic Specialty: College prep
Honors/Advanced Placement Classes: Yes
International Baccalaureate Program: No
Resources, Special Learning Needs: Yes
Profile: Est. 2003. Southeast side. Small school. Mandatory informa-
tion technology Education-to-Careers program. International stud-
ies enhanced with trips, foreign exchange programs, and model UN
classes.
Unique Traits: Thematic course of study
Public Transportation:
    CTA L: Red Line 87th
    CTA Bus: South Chicago
Dress Code: Navy or black slacks or skirt, school polo shirt
Admission Requirements: Priority given to students living in attendance
area; random lottery
Academic Scholarships: N/A

John Hancock High School

4034 West 56th Street Chicago, IL 60629
Phone Number: (773) 535-2410
Fax Number: (773) 535-2434

Web Site: www.cps.k12.il.us
E-mail: See Web site
Principal: Ms. Deborah Williams, Acting Principal
Admissions Contact: Mr. Joseph Jablonski
Gender: Coed

Total Enrollment: 600   *Student to Faculty Ratio:* 17:1
Number of Freshmen: 200   *Percentage of College Bound Grads:* 85%
Average Class Size: 28   *Tuition:* N/A

Other Expenditures: N/A
Academic Specialty: College prep
Honors/Advanced Placement Classes: Yes
International Baccalaureate Program: No
Resources, Special Learning Needs: Yes
Profile: Est. 1999. Westlawn. Small school. Group workshops and support programs. Leadership skills development program (partnership with the Bold Chicago Organization). Education-to-Careers program.
Unique Traits: Innovative college prep program
Public Transportation:
     CTA Bus: 79th, Cicero
Dress Code: Appropriate casual; jeans acceptable, white shirt with collar
Admission Requirements: Priority given to students living in attendance area
Academic Scholarships: N/A

John Marshall Harlan Community Academy

9652 South Michigan Avenue Chicago, IL 60628
Phone Number: (773) 535-5400
Fax Number: (773) 535-5061

Web Site: www.cps.k12.il.us
E-mail: See Web site
Principal: Dr. Gertrude Hill
Admissions Contact: Ms. Janet Williams
Gender: Coed

Total Enrollment: 1,386   *Student to Faculty Ratio:* 12:1
Number of Freshmen: 561   *Percentage of College Bound Grads:* 25%
Average Class Size: 28   *Tuition:* N/A

Other Expenditures: N/A
Academic Specialty: College prep
Honors/Advanced Placement Classes: Yes
International Baccalaureate Program: No
Resources, Special Learning Needs: Yes
Profile: Est. 1958. South side. Math, Science, and Technology Academy
    features state-of-the-art labs. After-school mentoring program. Edu-
    cation-to-Careers program. AVID program (rigorous college prep pro-
    gram for B and C students). JROTC.
Unique Traits: Program variety
Public Transportation:
    CTA Bus: Michigan
Dress Code: Appropriate casual; jeans acceptable
Admission Requirements: Priority given to students living in attendance
    area
Academic Scholarships: N/A

William Rainey Harper High School

6520 South Wood Street Chicago, IL 60636
Phone Number: (773) 535-9150
Fax Number: (773) 535-9090

Web Site: www.harper.cps.k12.il.us
E-mail: See Web site
Principal: Dr. Ron L. Gibbs
Admissions Contact: Ms. Catherine Radtke
Gender: Coed

Total Enrollment: 1,400   *Student to Faculty Ratio:* 15:1
Number of Freshmen: 500   *Percentage of College Bound Grads:* 20%
Average Class Size: 25–30   *Tuition:* N/A

Other Expenditures: N/A
Academic Specialty: College and career prep
Honors/Advanced Placement Classes: Yes
International Baccalaureate Program: No
Resources, Special Learning Needs: Yes
Profile: Est. 1911. West Englewood. Small school. Schools-within-a-school. Business organization partnerships provide students with career experience. Education-to-Careers programs. Language and Career Academy. JROTC.
Unique Traits: Leading participant in small schools movement
Public Transportation:
    CTA Bus: 63rd
Dress Code: Black slacks or skirt, white polo shirt
Admission Requirements: Priority given to students living in attendance area
Academic Scholarships: N/A

Hirsch Metropolitan High School
of Communications

7740 South Ingleside Avenue Chicago, IL 60619
Phone Number: (773) 535-3100
Fax Number: (773) 535-3240

Web Site: www.hirsch.cps.k12.il.us
E-mail: See Web site
Principal: Dr. Melverlene V. Parker
Admissions Contact: Ms. Linda G. Bailey
Gender: Coed

Total Enrollment: 700   *Student to Faculty Ratio:* 26:1
Number of Freshmen: 325   *Percentage of College Bound Grads:* 35%
Average Class Size: 24–28   *Tuition:* N/A

Other Expenditures: N/A
Academic Specialty: College prep
Honors/Advanced Placement Classes: Yes
International Baccalaureate Program: No
Resources, Special Learning Needs: Yes
Profile: Est. 1936. Chatham Avalon Park. Magnet school. Law and Public
   Safety Academy. Education-to-Careers programs.
Unique Traits: Specialized programs
Public Transportation:
   CTA *Bus:* Cottage Grove, 75th, 79th
Dress Code: Appropriate casual; no jeans
Admission Requirements: Accepts students citywide; random lottery
Academic Scholarships: N/A

John Hope College Preparatory High School

5515 South Lowe Avenue Chicago, IL 60621
Phone Number: (773) 535-3160
Fax Number: (773) 535-3444

Web Site: www.jhcp.cps.k12.il.us
E-mail: See Web site
Principal: Mr. Michael W. Durr
Admissions Contact: Ms. Carolyn Beasley-Jackson
Gender: Coed

Total Enrollment: 950   *Student to Faculty Ratio:* 27:1
Number of Freshmen: 340   *Percentage of College Bound Grads:* 95%
Average Class Size: 26   *Tuition:* N/A

Other Expenditures: N/A
Academic Specialty: College prep
Honors/Advanced Placement Classes: Yes
International Baccalaureate Program: No
Resources, Special Learning Needs: Yes
Profile: Est. 1972. Englewood. Grades 7–12. Magnet school. Academic
    Center (advanced program for 7th and 8th grades). Education-to-
    Careers program. Teacher teams identify specific student needs.
Unique Traits: Debate team won the city championship in 2003
Public Transportation:
    CTA Bus: Garfield
Dress Code: Khaki slacks, white or blue polo shirt
Admission Requirements: Accepts students citywide
Academic Scholarships: N/A

Gordon S. Hubbard High School

6200 South Hamlin Avenue Chicago, IL 60629
Phone Number: (773) 535-2200
Fax Number: (773) 535-2218

Web Site: www.hubbard.cps.k12.il.us
E-mail: See Web site
Principal: Mr. Andrew Manno
Admissions Contact: Ms. Emmer Shelton
Gender: Coed

Total Enrollment: 1,700   *Student to Faculty Ratio:* 21:1
Number of Freshmen: 400   *Percentage of College Bound Grads:* 80%
Average Class Size: 25   *Tuition:* N/A

Other Expenditures: N/A
Academic Specialty: College prep
Honors/Advanced Placement Classes: Yes
International Baccalaureate Program: Yes
Resources, Special Learning Needs: Yes
Profile: Est. 1965. Westlawn. Diverse student population. Education-to-Careers program. JROTC.
Unique Traits: 15 CPS Mock Trial championships. 2003 JROTC City Drill Platoon championship
Public Transportation:
     CTA Bus: Pulaski, 63rd
Dress Code: Black slacks or skirt, white polo shirt
Admission Requirements: Contact school
Academic Scholarships: N/A

Hyde Park Academy

6220 South Stony Island Avenue Chicago, IL 60637
Phone Number: (773) 535-0880
Fax Number: (773) 535-0633

Web Site: www.hydeparkhs.org
E-mail: See Web site
Principal: Ms. Dorothy C. Thomas
Admissions Contact: Ms. Austine Stuart
Gender: Coed

Total Enrollment: 1,800   *Student to Faculty Ratio:* 20:1
Number of Freshmen: 600   *Percentage of College Bound Grads:* 95%
Average Class Size: 17–18   *Tuition:* N/A

Other Expenditures: N/A
Academic Specialty: College and career prep
Honors/Advanced Placement Classes: Yes
International Baccalaureate Program: Yes
Resources, Special Learning Needs: Yes
Profile: Est. 1871. Hyde Park. Schools-within-a-school. Technology-based
curriculum. Education-to-Careers programs.
Unique Traits: Academic Decathlon has won 17 medals in the past 2
years
Public Transportation:
       CTA L: Green Line Cottage Grove
Dress Code: Appropriate casual; jeans acceptable
Admission Requirements: Priority given to students living in attendance
area
Academic Scholarships: N/A

Jones College Preparatory High School

606 South State Street Chicago, IL 60605
Phone Number: (773) 534-8600
Fax Number: (773) 534-8625

Web Site: www.jonescollegeprep.org
E-mail: admissions@jonescollegeprep.org
Principal: Dr. Donald Fraynd
Admissions Contact: Ms. Maureen Lai
Gender: Coed

Total Enrollment: 700	*Student to Faculty Ratio:* 21:1
Number of Freshmen: 150	*Percentage of College Bound Grads:* 100%
Average Class Size: 28	*Tuition:* N/A

Other Expenditures: N/A
Academic Specialty: College prep
Honors/Advanced Placement Classes: Yes
International Baccalaureate Program: No
Resources, Special Learning Needs: Yes
Profile: Est. 1998. South Loop. Selective Enrollment School. Rigorous academic program. State-of-the-art technology. College and university partnerships.
Unique Traits: Flat-screen computers in every classroom
Public Transportation:
>   CTA L: Red Line Harrison
>   CTA Bus: State
Dress Code: Appropriate casual; jeans acceptable
Admission Requirements: Accepts students citywide; entrance exam, transcripts
Academic Scholarships: N/A

Benito Juarez Community Academy

2150 South Laflin Street Chicago, IL 60608
Phone Number: (773) 534-7030
Fax Number: (773) 534-7058

Web Site: www.cps.k12.il.us
E-mail: See Web site
Principal: Mr. Natividad Loredo
Admissions Contact: Mr. Arturo Ortiz
Gender: Coed

Total Enrollment: 1,700   *Student to Faculty Ratio:* 20:1
Number of Freshmen: 500   *Percentage of College Bound Grads:* 35%
Average Class Size: 30   *Tuition:* N/A

Other Expenditures: N/A
Academic Specialty: College and career prep
Honors/Advanced Placement Classes: Yes
International Baccalaureate Program: No
Resources, Special Learning Needs: Yes
Profile: Est. 1972. Pilsen. Predominantly Mexican student population. Math, Science, and Technology Academy. JROTC. Education-to-Careers programs.
Unique Traits: Program variety
Public Transportation:
    CTA Bus: Ashland
Dress Code: Black slacks or skirt, white polo shirt
Admission Requirements: Contact school
Academic Scholarships: N/A

Percy L. Julian High School

10330 South Elizabeth Street Chicago, IL 60643
Phone Number: (773) 535-5170
Fax Number: (773) 535-2772

Web Site: www.pljulianhs.net
E-mail: See Web site
Principal: Mr. William Harris
Admissions Contact: Ms. Adrienne Walker-Alexander
Gender: Coed

Total Enrollment: 1,981
Student to Faculty Ratio: 20:1
Number of Freshmen: 608
Percentage of College Bound Grads: 55%
Average Class Size: 30
Tuition: N/A

Other Expenditures: N/A
Academic Specialty: College prep
Honors/Advanced Placement Classes: Yes
International Baccalaureate Program: No
Resources, Special Learning Needs: Yes
Profile: Est. 1975. Southwest side. Specialized medical and technical courses. Education-to-Careers programs. Medical Career Academy. Fine and Performing Arts Career Academy. World language programs.
Unique Traits: Thematic course of study
Public Transportation:
  CTA Bus: Vincennes, 103rd
Dress Code: Appropriate casual; jeans acceptable
Admission Requirements: Priority given to students living in attendance area
Academic Scholarships: N/A

Thomas Kelly High School

4136 South California Avenue Chicago, IL 60632
Phone Number: (773) 535-4900
Fax Number: (773) 535-4841

Web Site: www.kelly.cps.k12.il.us
E-mail: See Web site
Principal: Mr. Algird C. Pretkelis
Admissions Contact: Ms. Laura Jackson
Gender: Coed

Total Enrollment: 3,300   *Student to Faculty Ratio:* 20:1
Number of Freshmen: 1,100 *Percentage of College Bound Grads:* 75%
Average Class Size: 31   *Tuition:* N/A

Other Expenditures: N/A
Academic Specialty: College and career prep
Honors/Advanced Placement Classes: Yes
International Baccalaureate Program: Yes
Resources, Special Learning Needs: Yes
Profile: Est. 1933. Brighton Park. Magnet school. Metropolitan Studies.
    Education-to-Careers program. International Language and Career
    Academy. CISCO computer networking and certification.
Unique Traits: Named one of two CPS Improvement Project High Schools
Public Transportation:
    CTA Bus: Archer, California
Dress Code: Appropriate casual; jeans acceptable
Admission Requirements: Priority given to students living in attendance
    area
Academic Scholarships: N/A

Kelvyn Park High School

4343 West Wrightwood Avenue Chicago, IL 60639
Phone Number: (773) 534-4200
Fax Number: (773) 534-4507

Web Site: www.kelvynparkhs.org
E-mail: See Web site
Principal: Dr. Sandra Fontanez-Phelan
Admissions Contact: Ms. Aida Artuz
Gender: Coed

Total Enrollment: 1,750   *Student to Faculty Ratio:* 18:1
Number of Freshmen: 450   *Percentage of College Bound Grads:* 75%
Average Class Size: 28   *Tuition:* N/A

Other Expenditures: N/A
Academic Specialty: College and career prep
Honors/Advanced Placement Classes: Yes
International Baccalaureate Program: No
Resources, Special Learning Needs: Yes
Profile: Est. 1918. Kelvyn Park. Multiacademic options. Education-to-
    Careers program. Work Experience and Career Exploration programs.
    College Excel (early college credits). JROTC. Scholars program.
Unique Traits: Day and evening high school classes
Public Transportation:
    CTA Bus: Fullerton, Kostner
Dress Code: Blue slacks or skirt, white polo shirt
Admission Requirements: Priority given to students living in attendance
    area
Academic Scholarships: N/A

John F. Kennedy High School

6325 West 56th Street Chicago, IL 60638
Phone Number: (773) 535-2325
Fax Number: (773) 535-2485

Web Site: www.cps.k12.il.us
E-mail: See Web site
Principal: Mr. James Gorecki
Admissions Contact: Mr. Paul Lyons
Gender: Coed

Total Enrollment: 1,600	*Student to Faculty Ratio:* 15:1
Number of Freshmen: 450	*Percentage of College Bound Grads:* 60%
Average Class Size: 28	*Tuition:* N/A

Other Expenditures: N/A
Academic Specialty: College prep
Honors/Advanced Placement Classes: Yes
International Baccalaureate Program: No
Resources, Special Learning Needs: Yes
Profile: Est. 1962. Garfield Ridge. Range of programs offered for students of all abilities (autistic to gifted). Evening and Saturday classes available. Spanish and Polish bilingual programs. Technology Academy.
Unique Traits: Named a CPS "School of Merit" in 2003
Public Transportation:
      CTA Bus: Naragansett, Archer, 63rd
Dress Code: Navy blue slacks or skirt, white polo shirt
Admission Requirements: Students must live in attendance area
Academic Scholarships: N/A

Kenwood Academy

5015 South Blackstone Avenue Chicago, IL 60615
Phone Number: (773) 535-1350
Fax Number: (773) 535-1408

Web Site: www.kenwood.cps.k12.il.us
E-mail: See Web site
Principal: Mr. Arthur Slater
Admissions Contact: Ms. Camille Hamilton-Doyle
Gender: Coed

Total Enrollment: 1,700	*Student to Faculty Ratio:* 20:1
Number of Freshmen: 450	*Percentage of College Bound Grads:* 80%
Average Class Size: 28	*Tuition:* N/A

Other Expenditures: N/A
Academic Specialty: College and career prep
Honors/Advanced Placement Classes: Yes
International Baccalaureate Program: No
Resources, Special Learning Needs: Yes
Profile: Est. 1968. Hyde Park. Schools-within-a-school. Intensive mentoring programs. Education-to-Careers programs. Accelerated magnet program.
Unique Traits: Freshmen are divided into four communities based on academics
Public Transportation:
> CTA Bus: 51st
> Metra: 51st
Dress Code: Appropriate casual; jeans acceptable
Admission Requirements: Priority given to students living in attendance area
Academic Scholarships: N/A

Dr. Martin Luther King Jr. College Preparatory High School

4445 South Drexel Boulevard Chicago, IL 60653
Phone Number: (773) 535-1180
Fax Number: (773) 535-1658

Web Site: www.kinghs.cps.k12.il.us
E-mail: See Web site
Principal: Dr. Linda H. Coles
Admissions Contact: Mr. Kevin Tate
Gender: Coed

Total Enrollment: 200–500	*Student to Faculty Ratio:* 10:1
Number of Freshmen: 240	*Percentage of College Bound Grads:* N/A
Average Class Size: 28	*Tuition:* N/A

Other Expenditures: N/A
Academic Specialty: College and career prep
Honors/Advanced Placement Classes: Yes
International Baccalaureate Program: No
Resources, Special Learning Needs: Yes
Profile: Est. 2002. Kenwood. Selective Enrollment School. Integrated state-of-the-art technology and computer instruction. Education-to-Careers program.
Unique Traits: Students have placed first in city and state science and math competitions
Public Transportation:
      CTA Bus: Cottage Grove
Dress Code: Appropriate casual; jeans acceptable
Admission Requirements: Accepts students citywide: entrance exam, transcripts
Academic Scholarships: N/A

Lake View High School

4015 North Ashland Avenue Chicago, IL 60613
Phone Number: (773) 534-5440
Fax Number: (773) 534-5585

Web Site: www.lakeview.cps.k12.il.us
E-mail: See Web site
Principal: Mr. Scott Feaman
Admissions Contact: Ms. Jo Lipson
Gender: Coed

Total Enrollment: 1,250   *Student to Faculty Ratio:* 16:1
Number of Freshmen: 400   *Percentage of College Bound Grads:* 90%
Average Class Size: 25   *Tuition:* N/A

Other Expenditures: N/A
Academic Specialty: College prep
Honors/Advanced Placement Classes: Yes
International Baccalaureate Program: No
Resources, Special Learning Needs: Yes
Profile: Est. 1874. Lakeview. Math, Science, and Technology Academy.
   International Language and Career Academy. JROTC. Scholars pro-
   gram. Over 250 computer stations.
Unique Traits: Oldest high school in Illinois
Public Transportation:
        CTA L: Brown Line Irving Park
        CTA Bus: Irving Park, Ashland
Dress Code: Appropriate casual; jeans acceptable
Admission Requirements: Priority given to students living in attendance
   area
Academic Scholarships: N/A

Lane Tech College Prep High School

2501 West Addison Street Chicago, IL 60618
Phone Number: (773) 534-5400
Fax Number: (773) 534-5544

Web Site: www.lanetech.org
E-mail: See Web site
Principal: Mr. Keith Foley
Admissions Contact: Ms. Mollie Hart
Gender: Coed

Total Enrollment: 4,400   *Student to Faculty Ratio:* 28:1
Number of Freshmen: 1,100 *Percentage of College Bound Grads:* 92%
Average Class Size: 28   *Tuition:* N/A

Other Expenditures: N/A
Academic Specialty: College and career prep
Honors/Advanced Placement Classes: Yes
International Baccalaureate Program: No
Resources, Special Learning Needs: Yes
Profile: Est. 1908. Lakeview. Selective Enrollment School. 33-acre campus.
Offers honors, college core, technology, architecture/engineering, art,
and music programs. JROTC. Alpha program (scientific research).
Education-to-Careers programs.
Unique Traits: The largest high school in Illinois
Public Transportation:
    CTA Bus: Western, Addison
Dress Code: Appropriate casual; jeans acceptable
Admission Requirements: Accepts students citywide; entrance exam,
transcripts
Academic Scholarships: N/A

Las Casas Occupational High School

8 West Root Street Chicago, IL 60609
Phone Number: (773) 535-6050
Fax Number: (773) 535-6059

Web Site: www.cps.k12.il.us
E-mail: See Web site
Principal: Felix P. Winslow
Admissions Contact: Felix P. Winslow
Gender: Coed

Total Enrollment: 145
Number of Freshmen: 30
Average Class Size: 10

Student to Faculty Ratio: 9:1
Percentage of College Bound Grads: N/A
Tuition: N/A

Other Expenditures: N/A
Academic Specialty: Career prep
Honors/Advanced Placement Classes: No
International Baccalaureate Program: No
Resources, Special Learning Needs: Yes
Profile: Est. 1967. South side. A special education school for students ages 14–21 with autism and severe and profound emotional disabilities. On-site staffed clinic.
Unique Traits: The only public school that is a therapeutic day school
Public Transportation: School bus service provided based on student evaluation
Dress Code: Appropriate casual; jeans acceptable
Admission Requirements: Student evaluation
Academic Scholarships: N/A

Lincoln Park High School

2001 North Orchard Street Chicago, IL 60614
Phone Number: (773) 534-8130
Fax Number: (773) 534-8218

Web Site: www.lincolnpark.cps.k12.il.us
E-mail: See Web site
Principal: Dr. Bessie Karvelas
Admissions Contact: Ms. Jane Campbell
Gender: Coed

Total Enrollment: 2,200   *Student to Faculty Ratio:* 15:1
Number of Freshmen: 570   *Percentage of College Bound Grads:* 92%
Average Class Size: 28   *Tuition:* N/A

Other Expenditures: N/A
Academic Specialty: College prep
Honors/Advanced Placement Classes: Yes
International Baccalaureate Program: Yes
Resources, Special Learning Needs: Yes
Profile: Est. 1899. Lincoln Park. Three magnet programs: IB, Double Honors/
   AP, and Performing Arts. IB program ranked top 5% in the world. Top
   1% ranking in the U.S. for students taking AP and IB exams. Listed in
   Newsweek's "America's Best 100 Public High Schools," May 2005.
Unique Traits: Over the past 15 years, more National Merit semifinalists
   than all other CPS schools combined
Public Transportation:
   CTA L: Brown Line Armitage
   CTA Bus: Lincoln, Clark, Halsted
Dress Code: Appropriate casual; jeans acceptable
Admission Requirements: IB: 90%+ in reading and math; test, interview.
   Double Honors/AP: 76%+ in reading and math; no test, top 125 appli-
   cants chosen. Performing arts: 50%+ in reading and math; audition
Academic Scholarships: N/A

Robert Lindblom College Preparatory High School

6130 South Wolcott Chicago, IL 60644
Phone Number: (773) 535-9300
Fax Number: (773) 535-9314

Web Site: www.lindblom.cps.k12.il.us
E-mail: See Web site
Principal: Ms. W. Rean Sanders
Admissions Contact: Ms. Linda Miller
Gender: Coed

Total Enrollment: 520   *Student to Faculty Ratio:* 20:1
Number of Freshmen: 125   *Percentage of College Bound Grads:* 98%
Average Class Size: 24–28   *Tuition:* N/A

Other Expenditures: N/A
Academic Specialty: College and career prep
Honors/Advanced Placement Classes: Yes
International Baccalaureate Program: No
Resources, Special Learning Needs: Yes
Profile: Est. 1919. West Englewood. Selective Enrollment School. All classes are at the honors+ level. Award-winning JROTC. Education-to-Careers programs.
Unique Traits: Undergoing a $20 million renovation to create state-of-the-art lab facilities
Public Transportation:
      CTA Bus: 63rd
Dress Code: Khaki or black slacks or skirt, school polo shirt
Admission Requirements: Accepts freshmen students citywide: entrance exam, transcripts
Academic Scholarships: N/A

Hugh Manley Career Academy High School

2935 West Polk Street Chicago, IL 60612
Phone Number: (773) 534-6900
Fax Number: (773) 534-6924

Web Site: www.cps.k12.il.us
E-mail: See Web site
Principal: Dr. Katherine Flanagan
Admissions Contact: Ms. Juanita Henderson
Gender: Coed

Total Enrollment: 700   *Student to Faculty Ratio:* 17:1
Number of Freshmen: 300   *Percentage of College Bound Grads:* 70%
Average Class Size: 28   *Tuition:* N/A

Other Expenditures: N/A
Academic Specialty: College and career prep
Honors/Advanced Placement Classes: Yes
International Baccalaureate Program: No
Resources, Special Learning Needs: Yes
Profile: Est. 1926. North Lawndale. Schools-within-a-school. 100% African American student body. Students choose a career cluster after freshman year: construction, culinary arts, medical arts, business technology, or graphic design.
Unique Traits: Combines academics with a career prep program (site visits, job shadowing)
Public Transportation:
   CTA Bus: California, Harrison, Roosevelt
Dress Code: Black or navy slacks or skirt, school polo shirt
Admission Requirements: Priority given to students living in attendance area
Academic Scholarships: N/A

John Marshall Metropolitan High School

3250 West Adams Street Chicago, IL 60624
Phone Number: (773) 534-6455
Fax Number: (773) 534-6409

Web Site: www.cps.k12.il.us
E-mail: See Web site
Principal: Dr. Gwendolyn Boyd
Admissions Contact: Ms. Leslie Archibald
Gender: Coed

Total Enrollment: 2,000   *Student to Faculty Ratio:* 21:1
Number of Freshmen: 375   *Percentage of College Bound Grads:* 80%
Average Class Size: 28   *Tuition:* N/A

Other Expenditures: N/A
Academic Specialty: College and career prep
Honors/Advanced Placement Classes: Yes
International Baccalaureate Program: No
Resources, Special Learning Needs: Yes
Profile: Est. 1895. West side. School-within-a-school. Serving low-income students. Education-to-Careers program. Academy of Finance.
Unique Traits: Chicago Reading Initiative: daily reading and writing instruction across the curriculum
Public Transportation:
    CTA Bus: Jackson
Dress Code: Appropriate casual; jeans acceptable
Admission Requirements: Priority given to students living in attendance area
Academic Scholarships: N/A

Stephen Tyng Mather High School

5835 North Lincoln Avenue Chicago, IL 60659
Phone Number: (773) 534-2350
Fax Number: (773) 534-2424

Web Site: www.cps.k12.il.us
E-mail: See Web site
Principal: Mr. John A. Butterfield
Admissions Contact: Ms. Marta Wortman
Gender: Coed

Total Enrollment: 1,960   *Student to Faculty Ratio:* 17:1
Number of Freshmen: 500   *Percentage of College Bound Grads:* 90%
Average Class Size: 28   *Tuition:* N/A

Other Expenditures: N/A
Academic Specialty: College and career prep
Honors/Advanced Placement Classes: Yes
International Baccalaureate Program: No
Resources, Special Learning Needs: Yes
Profile: Est. 1968. Peterson Park. Multicultural, multilingual student population. Faculty and staff serve as translators, role models, and mentors. Vocational education programs.
Unique Traits: Bilingual English-as-a-Second-Language program
Public Transportation:
        CTA Bus: Lincoln, Peterson
Dress Code: Appropriate casual; jeans acceptable
Admission Requirements: Priority given to students living in attendance area; random lottery
Academic Scholarships: N/A

Morgan Park High School

1744 West Pryor Avenue Chicago, IL 60643
Phone Number: (773) 535-2550
Fax Number: (773) 535-2706

Web Site: www.morganpark.cps.org
E-mail: See Web site
Principal: Dr. Beryl Shingles
Admissions Contact: Ms. Dorothy Connie
Gender: Coed

Total Enrollment: 2,357   *Student to Faculty Ratio:* 25:1
Number of Freshmen: 668   *Percentage of College Bound Grads:* 85%
Average Class Size: 28   *Tuition:* N/A

Other Expenditures: N/A
Academic Specialty: College and career prep
Honors/Advanced Placement Classes: Yes
International Baccalaureate Program: Yes
Resources, Special Learning Needs: Yes
Profile: Est. 1916. Southwest side. 25-acre campus. Education-to-Careers programs. Academic Center (rigorous program). World Language and International Studies magnet program.
Unique Traits: Named CPS Athletic School of the year in 2003. Debate team won first place in Chicago
Public Transportation:
    CTA Bus: 111th, Vincennes
Dress Code: Appropriate casual; jeans acceptable
Admission Requirements: Call school
Academic Scholarships: N/A

New Millennium School of Health

2710 East 89th Street Chicago, IL 60617
Phone Number: (773) 535-7650
Fax Number: (773) 535-6489

Web Site: www.nmsh.cps.k12.il.us
E-mail: See Web site
Principal: Ms. Arlana Bedard
Admissions Contact: Ms. Helen Johnson-Collins
Gender: Coed

Total Enrollment: 248–400 *Student to Faculty Ratio:* 10:1
Number of Freshmen: 139 *Percentage of College Bound Grads:* N/A
Average Class Size: 24 *Tuition:* N/A

Other Expenditures: N/A
Academic Specialty: College prep
Honors/Advanced Placement Classes: Yes
International Baccalaureate Program: No
Resources, Special Learning Needs: Yes
Profile: Est. 2004. Southeast side. Small school located in the Bowen campus. Rigorous program with an emphasis on health, math, and science. Specialized programs; students work alongside health professionals.
Unique Traits: Thematic course of study
Public Transportation:
        CTA L: Red Line 87th
        CTA Bus: South Chicago
Dress Code: Black or dark blue slacks or skirt, school polo shirt
Admission Requirements: Priority given to students living in attendance area; random lottery
Academic Scholarships: N/A

Noble Street Charter High School

1010 North Noble Street Chicago, IL 60622
Phone Number: (773) 862-1449
Fax Number: (773) 278-0421

Web Site: www.goldentigers.org
E-mail: mmilkie@ goldentigers.org
Principal: Mr. Michael Milkie
Admissions Contact: Mr. Michael Milkie
Gender: Coed

Total Enrollment: 480   *Student to Faculty Ratio:* 15:1
Number of Freshmen: 160   *Percentage of College Bound Grads:* 80%
Average Class Size: 20   *Tuition:* N/A

Other Expenditures: N/A
Academic Specialty: College prep
Honors/Advanced Placement Classes: Yes
International Baccalaureate Program: No
Resources, Special Learning Needs: Yes
Profile: Est. 1999. West Town. Small school located in the Northwestern
  University Settlement House. Strong curriculum. College programs
  offered.
Unique Traits: Run like a private school in terms of discipline and dress
  code.
Public Transportation:
  CTA L: Blue Line Division
  CTA Bus: Milwaukee
Dress Code: Khaki slacks, school polo shirt
Admission Requirements: Accepts students citywide; lottery
Academic Scholarships: N/A

North Grand High School

4338 West Wabansia Avenue Chicago, IL 60639
Phone Number: (773) 534-8520
Fax Number: (773) 534-8535

Web Site: www.cps.k12.il.us
E-mail: See Web site
Principal: Dr. Asuncion A. Ayala
Admissions Contact: Ms. Vaccarezza Isla
Gender: Coed

Total Enrollment: 506–800 *Student to Faculty Ratio:* 28:1
Number of Freshmen: 252 *Percentage of College Bound Grads:* N/A
Average Class Size: 27 *Tuition:* N/A

Other Expenditures: N/A
Academic Specialty: College and career prep
Honors/Advanced Placement Classes: Yes
International Baccalaureate Program: No
Resources, Special Learning Needs: Yes
Profile: Est. 2004. West Humboldt Park. Career Exploration program. Education-to-Careers programs. Block scheduling. In year two, students choose their course of study: Scholars Program, media production, architecture, Allied Health, or culinary arts.
Unique Traits: Bilingual student population (Spanish)
Public Transportation:
    CTA Bus: Kostner, North
Dress Code: Professional business attire; no jeans
Admission Requirements: Priority is given to students living in attendance area
Academic Scholarships: N/A

North Lawndale College Preparatory Charter High School

1616 South Spaulding Avenue Chicago, IL 60623
Phone Number: (773) 542-1490
Fax Number: (773) 542-1492

Web Site: www.nlcphs.org
E-mail: See Web site
Principal: Mr. John Horan, Dean of Students
Admissions Contact: Mr. Chris Kelly
Gender: Coed

Total Enrollment: 370   *Student to Faculty Ratio:* 21:1
Number of Freshmen: 85   *Percentage of College Bound Grads:* 90%
Average Class Size: 17–23   *Tuition:* N/A

Other Expenditures: N/A
Academic Specialty: College prep
Honors/Advanced Placement Classes: Yes
International Baccalaureate Program: No
Resources, Special Learning Needs: Yes
Profile: Est. 1998. North Lawndale. Small school. Serving low-income students. Combines community service and work experience with academics. A counselor/social worker is assigned to each freshmen class through their first year of college.
Unique Traits: Recipient of three Golden Apple Teaching Award nominations
Public Transportation:
    CTA Bus: 16th
Dress Code: Khaki slacks, white polo shirt
Admission Requirements: Accepts students citywide; random lottery
Academic Scholarships: N/A

Northside College Preparatory High School

5501 North Kedzie Avenue Chicago, IL 60625
Phone Number: (773) 534-3954
Fax Number: (773) 534-3964

Web Site: www.northsideprep.org
E-mail: crownd@northsideprep.org
Principal: Dr. James C. Lalley
Admissions Contact: Ms. Carolyn Rownd
Gender: Coed

Total Enrollment: 1,000   *Student to Faculty Ratio:* 21:1
Number of Freshmen: 250   *Percentage of College Bound Grads:* 99%
Average Class Size: 18–28   *Tuition:* N/A

Other Expenditures: N/A
Academic Specialty: College prep
Honors/Advanced Placement Classes: Yes
International Baccalaureate Program: No
Resources, Special Learning Needs: Yes
Profile: Est. 1999. Albany Park. Selective Enrollment School. Rigorous curriculum; all classes are at an honors+ level. Liberal arts emphasis in a technology-rich environment. Colloquium program. Block scheduling. Presented the Siemens Award in 2002, granted to 12 high schools nationally for increased enrollment in AP math and science courses.
Unique Traits: Highest scores on Illinois Prairie State Exam of any high school in 2001, 2002, 2003, and 2004; impressive facility
Public Transportation:
   CTA L: Brown Line Kimball
   Bus: Northside shuttle bus available at an extra cost (call school for routes)
Dress Code: Appropriate casual; jeans acceptable
Admission Requirements: Accepts students citywide; entrance exam, transcripts
Academic Scholarships: N/A

Walter Payton College Preparatory High School

1034 North Wells Street Chicago, IL 60610
Phone Number: (773) 534-0034
Fax Number: (773) 534-0035

Web Site: www.wpcp.org
E-mail: See Web site
Principal: Ms. Gail Ward
Admissions Contact: Ms. Sandrai Stigler
Gender: Coed

Total Enrollment: 800   *Student to Faculty Ratio:* 25:1
Number of Freshmen: 200   *Percentage of College Bound Grads:* 98%
Average Class Size: 15–28   *Tuition:* N/A

Other Expenditures: N/A
Academic Specialty: College prep
Honors/Advanced Placement Classes: Yes
International Baccalaureate Program: No
Resources, Special Learning Needs: Yes
Profile: Est. 2000. Old Town. Selective Enrollment School. All classes are at an honors+ level. Rooftop planetarium and greenhouse. Leadership training classes. Videoconference center.
Unique Traits: High Illinois Prairie State Exam scores, impressive facility
Public Transportation:
    CTA L: Red Line Chicago, Brown Line Chicago
    CTA Bus: Chicago, LaSalle
Dress Code: Appropriate casual; no jeans
Admission Requirements: Accepts freshmen students citywide; entrance exam, transcripts
Academic Scholarships: N/A

Wendell Phillips Academy High School

244 East Pershing Road Chicago, IL 60653
Phone Number: (773) 535-1603
Fax Number: (773) 535-1605

Web Site: www.cps.k12.il.us
E-mail: See Web site
Principal: Mr. Euel Benton
Admissions Contact: Mr. Lenton Kirkland
Gender: Coed

Total Enrollment: 755   *Student to Faculty Ratio:* 10:1
Number of Freshmen: 200   *Percentage of College Bound Grads:* 45%
Average Class Size: 20   *Tuition:* N/A

Other Expenditures: N/A
Academic Specialty: College and career prep
Honors/Advanced Placement Classes: Yes
International Baccalaureate Program: No
Resources, Special Learning Needs: Yes
Profile: Est. 1904. Bronzeville. Rigorous academic curriculum. Math, Science, and Technology Academy. JROTC. Education-to-Careers programs.
Unique Traits: Partnerships with community organizations and universities
Public Transportation:
     CTA Bus: King, State, Michigan
Dress Code: Navy blue slacks or skirt, white polo shirt
Admission Requirements: Priority given to students living in attendance area. Academy and JROTC accept students citywide
Academic Scholarships: N/A

Phoenix Military Academy

145 South Campbell Avenue Chicago, IL 60612
Phone Number: (773) 534-7275
Fax Number: (773) 534-7273

Web Site: www.phoenixmilitary.org
E-mail: See Web site
Principal: Mr. Ferdinand Wipachit
Admissions Contact: Mr. Tim Craddock
Gender: Coed

Total Enrollment: 350   *Student to Faculty Ratio:* 15:1
Number of Freshmen: 150   *Percentage of College Bound Grads:* N/A
Average Class Size: 25   *Tuition:* N/A

Other Expenditures: N/A
Academic Specialty: College prep
Honors/Advanced Placement Classes: Yes
International Baccalaureate Program: No
Resources, Special Learning Needs: Yes
Profile: Est. 2004. West Humboldt Park. Combines academics with JROTC
   training. Structured atmosphere.
Unique Traits: Military academy
Public Transportation:
        CTA L: Blue Line
        CTA Bus: Western
Dress Code: Standard military uniform
Admission Requirements: Random lottery
Academic Scholarships: N/A

Charles A. Prosser Career Academy

2148 North Long Avenue Chicago, IL 60639
Phone Number: (773) 534-3200
Fax Number: (773) 534-3382

Web Site: www.prosser.cps.k12.il.us
E-mail: See Web site
Principal: Mr. Kenneth L. Hunter
Admissions Contact: Ms. Ella Austin
Gender: Coed

Total Enrollment: 1,365	*Student to Faculty Ratio:* 20:1
Number of Freshmen: 350	*Percentage of College Bound Grads:* 70%
Average Class Size: 20–25	*Tuition:* N/A

Other Expenditures: N/A
Academic Specialty: College and career prep
Honors/Advanced Placement Classes: Yes
International Baccalaureate Program: Yes
Resources, Special Learning Needs: Yes
Profile: Est. 1958. Northwest side. Freshman Academy eases first year transition. Sophomores choose between the IB or the Education-to-Careers programs. Spanish and Polish bilingual programs.
Unique Traits: Impressive number of Merit and Illinois State Scholars.
Public Transportation:
      CTA Bus: Grand, Central
Dress Code: Appropriate casual; jeans acceptable
Admission Requirements: Priority given to students living in attendance area
Academic Scholarships: N/A

Al Raby High School for Community and Environment

3545 West Fulton Boulevard Chicago, IL 60624
Phone Number: (773) 534-6755
Fax Number: (773) 534-6938

Web Site: www.alraby.cps.k12.il.us
E-mail: See Web site
Principal: Ms. Janice Jackson
Admissions Contact: Mr. Randy Twilley
Gender: Coed

Total Enrollment: 125–500   *Student to Faculty Ratio:* 15:1
Number of Freshmen: 125   *Percentage of College Bound Grads:* N/A
Average Class Size: 16   *Tuition:* N/A

Other Expenditures: N/A
Academic Specialty: College prep
Honors/Advanced Placement Classes: Yes
International Baccalaureate Program: No
Resources, Special Learning Needs: Yes
Profile: Est. 2004. Garfield Park. Small school. State-of-the-art environmental program. Community internships as part of the school day. Geographic Information System (GIS) mapping technology utilized.
Unique Traits: Thematic course of study
Public Transportation:
    CTA L: Green Line Conservatory
    CTA Bus: Fulton
Dress Code: Appropriate casual; jeans acceptable
Admission Requirements: Accepts students citywide
Academic Scholarships: N/A

Mirta Ramirez Computer Science Charter School

2435 North Western Avenue Chicago, IL 60647
Phone Number: (773) 252-6662
Fax Number: (773) 252-0994

Web Site: www.aspirail.org/mrcscs.htm
E-mail: See Web site
Principal: Ms. Patricia Munoz-Rocha
Admissions Contact: Mr. Leyner Argueta
Gender: Coed

Total Enrollment: 260–500   *Student to Faculty Ratio:* 19:1
Number of Freshmen: 100   *Percentage of College Bound Grads:* N/A
Average Class Size: 20–25   *Tuition:* N/A

Other Expenditures: N/A
Academic Specialty: Career prep
Honors/Advanced Placement Classes: No
International Baccalaureate Program: No
Resources, Special Learning Needs: Yes
Profile: Est. 2003. Logan Square. Computer technology focus for inner-city youth. Sponsored by Aspira, a Puerto Rican not-for-profit organization dedicated to Latino education and leadership. Two years of general study, two years of study within the computer field. Local business internships.
Unique Traits: Students graduate with the equivalent of an Associate Degree in Computer Technology
Public Transportation:
    CTA Bus: Western
Dress Code: Khaki slacks, school polo shirt
Admission Requirements: Accepts students citywide; random lottery
Academic Scholarships: N/A

Ellen H. Richards Career Academy High School

5009 South Laflin Street Chicago, IL 60609
Phone Number: (773) 535-4945
Fax Number: (773) 535-4883

Web Site: www.cps.k12.il.us
E-mail: See Web site
Principal: Dr. Joyce O. Smith
Admissions Contact: Ms. Maryanne Czerwinski
Gender: Coed

Total Enrollment: 515   *Student to Faculty Ratio:* 19:1
Number of Freshmen: 150   *Percentage of College Bound Grads:* 65%
Average Class Size: 20–22   *Tuition:* N/A

Other Expenditures: N/A
Academic Specialty: Career prep
Honors/Advanced Placement Classes: Yes
International Baccalaureate Program: No
Resources, Special Learning Needs: Yes
Profile: Est. 1991. New City. Mandatory Computer Information Technology program required. Education-to-Careers programs.
Unique Traits: $3 million renovation recently completed
Public Transportation:
        CTA Bus: Ashland
Dress Code: Black slacks or skirt, white polo shirt
Admission Requirements: Accepts students citywide
Academic Scholarships: N/A

Paul Robeson High School

6835 South Normal Boulevard Chicago, IL 60621
Phone Number: (773) 535-3800
Fax Number: (773) 535-3620

Web Site: www.robeson.cps.k12.il.us
E-mail: See Web site
Principal: Mr. James E. Breashears
Admissions Contact: Mr. Curtis Bishop
Gender: Coed

Total Enrollment: 1,030   *Student to Faculty Ratio:* 18:1
Number of Freshmen: 300   *Percentage of College Bound Grads:* 65%
Average Class Size: 28   *Tuition:* N/A

Other Expenditures: N/A
Academic Specialty: College and career prep
Honors/Advanced Placement Classes: Yes
International Baccalaureate Program: No
Resources, Special Learning Needs: Yes
Profile: Est. 1976. Englewood. AVID program (rigorous curriculum for B and C students. Mentoring, job shadowing, and internships. Math, Science, and Technology Academy. International Career and Language Academy.
Unique Traits: Program variety
Public Transportation:
    CTA Bus: Normal
Dress Code: Navy blue slacks or skirt, white polo shirt
Admission Requirements: Contact school
Academic Scholarships: N/A

Theodore Roosevelt High School

3436 West Wilson Avenue Chicago, IL 60625
Phone Number: (773) 534-5000
Fax Number: (773) 534-5044

Web Site: www.roosevelt.cps.k12.il.us
E-mail: See Web site
Principal: Dr. Alejandra Alvarez
Admissions Contact: Mr. William Meyer
Gender: Coed

Total Enrollment: 1,670   *Student to Faculty Ratio:* 17:1
Number of Freshmen: 350   *Percentage of College Bound Grads:* 60%
Average Class Size: 25   *Tuition:* N/A

Other Expenditures: N/A
Academic Specialty: College and career prep
Honors/Advanced Placement Classes: Yes
International Baccalaureate Program: No
Resources, Special Learning Needs: Yes
Profile: Est. 1932. Albany Park. Ethnically and culturally diverse. Education-to-Careers programs. JROTC. Math, Science, and Technology Academy. Impressive list of student awards.
Unique Traits: Relationships with a robotic club and Princeton University
Public Transportation:
    CTA L: Brown Line Wilson
Dress Code: Appropriate casual; jeans acceptable
Admission Requirements: Priority given to students living in attendance area. Academies: contact school
Academic Scholarships: N/A

School of the Arts High School

7529 South Constance Avenue Chicago, IL 60649
Phone Number: (773) 535-6180 Ext. 101
Fax Number: (773) 535-6088

Web Site: www.cps.k12.il.us
E-mail: See Web site
Principal: Mr. Douglas Macklin
Admissions Contact: Dr. Lois M. Gueno
Gender: Coed

Total Enrollment: 400–500
Student to Faculty Ratio: 17:1
Number of Freshmen: 100
Percentage of College Bound Grads: N/A
Average Class Size: 29
Tuition: N/A

Other Expenditures: N/A
Academic Specialty: College and career prep
Honors/Advanced Placement Classes: Yes
International Baccalaureate Program: No
Resources, Special Learning Needs: Yes
Profile: Est. 2002. South Shore. Small school located in the South Shore campus. Visual and performing arts curriculum enhanced by community art groups and artists in residence.
Unique Traits: Thematic course of study
Public Transportation:
 CTA Bus: 76th
 Metra: Jeffrey
Dress Code: Appropriate casual; jeans acceptable, school shirt
Admission Requirements: Priority given to students living in attendance area; random lottery
Academic Scholarships: N/A

School of Entrepreneurship High School

7627 South Constance Avenue Chicago, IL 60649
Phone Number: (773) 535-6190 Ext. 137
Fax Number: (773) 535-6960

Web Site: www.cps.k12.il.us
E-mail: See Web site
Principal: Mr. William Gerstein
Admissions Contact: Ms. Pam Warner
Gender: Coed

Total Enrollment: 360–500   *Student to Faculty Ratio:* 12:1
Number of Freshmen: 130   *Percentage of College Bound Grads:* N/A
Average Class Size: 25   *Tuition:* N/A

Other Expenditures: N/A
Academic Specialty: College and career prep
Honors/Advanced Placement Classes: Yes
International Baccalaureate Program: No
Resources, Special Learning Needs: Yes
Profile: Est. 2002. South Shore. Small school located in the South Shore
Campus. Business and service-oriented curriculum. Local business
internships. Student owned and operated business.
Unique Traits: Thematic course of study
Public Transportation:
    CTA Bus: 76th
    Metra: Jeffrey
Dress Code: Appropriate casual; jeans acceptable, school shirt
Admission Requirements: Priority given to students living in attendance
area; random lottery
Academic Scholarships: N/A

School of Leadership High School

7627 South Constance Avenue Chicago, IL 60649
Phone Number: (773) 535-6190 Ext. 108
Fax Number: (773) 535-6960

Web Site: www.cps.k12.il.us
E-mail: See Web site
Principal: Mr. James E. Patrick
Admissions Contact: Ms. Ann McCool
Gender: Coed

Total Enrollment: 360–500   *Student to Faculty Ratio:* 20:1
Number of Freshmen: 150   *Percentage of College Bound Grads:* N/A
Average Class Size: 28   *Tuition:* N/A

Other Expenditures: N/A
Academic Specialty: College and career prep
Honors/Advanced Placement Classes: Yes
International Baccalaureate Program: No
Resources, Special Learning Needs: Yes
Profile: Est. 2003. South Shore. Small school located in the South Shore Campus. Mandatory JROTC program offers criminal justice and political science courses. Partnership with Chicago State University.
Unique Traits: The Peer Jury program enables students to be jurors for real juvenile court cases.
Public Transportation:
    CTA Bus: 76th
    Metra: Jeffrey
Dress Code: Appropriate casual; jeans acceptable, school polo shirt
Admission Requirements: Preference given to students living in attendance area; random lottery
Academic Scholarships: N/A

School of Technology High School

7627 South Constance Avenue Chicago, IL 60649
Phone Number: (773) 535-6180 Ext. 104
Fax Number: (773) 535-6088

Web Site: www.cps.k12.il.us
E-mail: See Web site
Principal: Dr. Olufemi Adeniji
Admissions Contact: Ms. Rita Adams-Hawkins
Gender: Coed

Total Enrollment: 285–500   *Student to Faculty Ratio:* 16:1
Number of Freshmen: 150   *Percentage of College Bound Grads:* N/A
Average Class Size: 18–36   *Tuition:* N/A

Other Expenditures: N/A
Academic Specialty: College and career prep
Honors/Advanced Placement Classes: Yes
International Baccalaureate Program: No
Resources, Special Learning Needs: Yes
Profile: Est. 2003. South Shore. Small school located in the South Shore
   campus. Computer and information science career prep. Education-
   to-Careers programs for industry certification. On-site internship
   programs.
Unique Traits: Thematic course of study
Public Transportation:
   CTA Bus: 76th
   Metra: Jeffery
Dress Code: Navy blue slacks or skirt, collared shirt
Admission Requirements: Priority given to students living in attendance
   area; random lottery
Academic Scholarships: N/A

Carl Schurz High School

3601 North Milwaukee Avenue Chicago, IL 60641
Phone Number: (773) 534-3420
Fax Number: (773) 534-3573

Web Site: www.schurz.cps.k12.il.us
E-mail: See Web site
Principal: Sharon Rae Bender, PhD
Admissions Contact: Ms. Sol M. Rodriguez
Gender: Coed

Total Enrollment: 2,600   *Student to Faculty Ratio:* 17:1
Number of Freshmen: 1,059   *Percentage of College Bound Grads:* 40%
Average Class Size: 28   *Tuition:* N/A

Other Expenditures: N/A
Academic Specialty: College and career prep
Honors/Advanced Placement Classes: Yes
International Baccalaureate Program: No
Resources, Special Learning Needs: Yes
Profile: Est. 1910. Jeffrey Park. Academy of Finance. Academy of Fine and Performing Arts. Education-to-Careers programs.
Unique Traits: In 2003 received the Grand Award, Newhouse Competition in Architectural Drafting, and the Scholastic Press Association's Superior Overall Newspaper Award
Public Transportation:
    CTA Bus: Milwaukee, Addison
Dress Code: Navy blue slacks or skirt, white polo shirt
Admission Requirements: Priority given to students living in attendance area. Academies: accepts freshman students citywide
Academic Scholarships: N/A

Nicholas Senn High School

5900 North Glenwood Avenue Chicago, IL 60660
Phone Number: (773) 534-2365
Fax Number: (773) 534-2369

Web Site: www.sennhighschool.org
E-mail: See Web site
Principal: Mr. Richard S. Norman
Admissions Contact: Ms. Mary Pat McKenna
Gender: Coed

Total Enrollment: 1,500   *Student to Faculty Ratio:* 17:1
Number of Freshmen: 470   *Percentage of College Bound Grads:* 80%
Average Class Size: 25   *Tuition:* N/A

Other Expenditures: N/A
Academic Specialty: College and career prep
Honors/Advanced Placement Classes: Yes
International Baccalaureate Program: Yes
Resources, Special Learning Needs: Yes
Profile: Est. 1913. Edgewater. Diverse student population. Programs for
   both advanced and struggling students. Bilingual program. Education-
   to-Careers programs.
Unique Traits: The Environmental and Spatial Technology Initiative utilize
   state-of-the-art technology.
Public Transportation:
   CTA L: Red Line Thorndale
Dress Code: Khaki, navy, or black slacks or skirt; white shirt
Admission Requirements: Contact the school
Academic Scholarships: N/A

Neal F. Simeon Career Academy High School

8147 South Vincennes Avenue Chicago, IL 60620
Phone Number: (773) 535-3200
Fax Number: (773) 535-3465

Web Site: www.cps.k12.il.us
E-mail: See Web site
Principal: Mr. John Everett
Admissions Contact: Ms. Denise Bournique
Gender: Coed

Total Enrollment: 1,560   *Student to Faculty Ratio:* 20:1
Number of Freshmen: 400   *Percentage of College Bound Grads:* 50%
Average Class Size: 28   *Tuition:* N/A

Other Expenditures: N/A
Academic Specialty: College and career prep
Honors/Advanced Placement Classes: Yes
International Baccalaureate Program: No
Resources, Special Learning Needs: Yes
Profile: Est. 1964. South side. Moved to a new state-of-the-art building
   in 2003. General course of study first two years, then must choose an
   Education-to-Careers program. Inroads program (college guidance).
   JROTC.
Unique Traits: Mandatory curriculum
Public Transportation:
      CTA Bus: Vincennes
Dress Code: Appropriate casual; jeans acceptable
Admission Requirements: Accepts students citywide
Academic Scholarships: N/A

Southside Occupational Academy

7342 South Hoyne Avenue Chicago, IL 60636
Phone Number: (773) 535-9100
Fax Number: (773) 535-9110

Web Site: www.southside.cps.k12.il.us
E-mail: See Web site
Principal: Ms. Gwendolyn A. Mims
Admissions Contact: Ms. Mary Pat O'Connor
Gender: Coed

Total Enrollment: 232   *Student to Faculty Ratio:* 10:1
Number of Freshmen: N/A   *Percentage of College Bound Grads:* N/A
Average Class Size: 10–12   *Tuition:* N/A

Other Expenditures: N/A
Academic Specialty: Career prep
Honors/Advanced Placement Classes: No
International Baccalaureate Program: No
Resources, Special Learning Needs: Yes
Profile: Est. 1960. South side. Grades 9–12. Entry-level vocational training for students 16–21 years old with moderate to severe cognitive disabilities. Each student is charted and assessed to evaluate their progress.
Unique Traits: Specializing in the special needs student
Public Transportation:
    CTA Bus: Damen
Dress Code: Dark slacks or skirt, white shirt
Admission Requirements: Students must live within attendance area and have completed two years of high school
Academic Scholarships: N/A

Charles P. Steinmetz Academic Centre

3030 North Mobile Avenue Chicago, IL 60634
Phone Number: (773) 534-3030
Fax Number: (773) 534-3151

Web Site: www.steinmetzac.com
E-mail: See Web site
Principal: Dr. Eunice Madon
Admissions Contact: Ms. Corrine Myers
Gender: Coed

Total Enrollment: 2,700   *Student to Faculty Ratio:* 19:1
Number of Freshmen: 450   *Percentage of College Bound Grads:* 40%
Average Class Size: 20–28   *Tuition:* N/A

Other Expenditures: N/A
Academic Specialty: College and career prep
Honors/Advanced Placement Classes: Yes
International Baccalaureate Program: Yes
Resources, Special Learning Needs: Yes
Profile: Est. 1935. Northwest side. All levels of academic programs. International Language and Career Academy. JROTC. Work Experience Career Exploration program.
Unique Traits: The Academic Decathlon Team has won gold, silver, and bronze medals in citywide competitions
Public Transportation:
    CTA Bus: Diversity, Belmont, Naragansett
Dress Code: Appropriate casual; jeans acceptable. JROTC: standard government military uniform
Admission Requirements: Call school
Academic Scholarships: N/A

Roger C. Sullivan High School

6631 North Bosworth Avenue Chicago, IL 60626
Phone Number:(773) 534-2000
Fax Number: (773) 534-2141

Web Site: www.sullivanhs.org
E-mail: See Web site
Principal: Mr. Andrew D. Rowlas
Admissions Contact: Mr. Craig Hahn
Gender: Coed

Total Enrollment: 1,200   *Student to Faculty Ratio:* 15:1
Number of Freshmen: 540   *Percentage of College Bound Grads:* 75%
Average Class Size: 28   *Tuition:* N/A

Other Expenditures: N/A
Academic Specialty: College and career prep
Honors/Advanced Placement Classes: Yes
International Baccalaureate Program: No
Resources, Special Learning Needs: Yes
Profile: Est. 1925. Rogers Park. Schools-within-a-school. Culturally diverse. Medical and Health Career Academy. Paideia program.
Unique Traits: Students and their families speak more than 35 languages
Public Transportation:
        CTA Bus: Clark
Dress Code: Appropriate casual; jeans acceptable
Admission Requirements: Priority to students living in attendance area
Academic Scholarships: N/A

William Howard Taft High School

6530 West Bryn Mawr Avenue Chicago, IL 60631
Phone Number: (773) 534-1000
Fax Number: (773) 534-1027

Web Site: www.tafths.org
E-mail: See Web site
Principal: Dr. Arthur Tarvardian
Admissions Contact: Ms. Phyllis Ehret
Gender: Coed

Total Enrollment: 1,800	*Student to Faculty Ratio:* 17:1
Number of Freshmen: 800	*Percentage of College Bound Grads:* 75%
Average Class Size: 28	*Tuition:* N/A

Other Expenditures: N/A
Academic Specialty: College prep
Honors/Advanced Placement Classes: Yes
International Baccalaureate Program: Yes
Resources, Special Learning Needs: Yes
Profile: Est. 1948. Norwood Park. Academic Center for gifted 7th and 8th graders. Education-to-Careers programs.
Unique Traits: JROTC (navy) ranked in nation's top 10
Public Transportation:
    CTA Bus: Nagle
Dress Code: Blue or black slacks, white shirt with collar. JROTC: standard government military uniform
Admission Requirements: Priority given to students living in attendance. IB, JROTC: call school
Academic Scholarships: N/A

Edward Tilden Career Community Academy

4747 South Union Avenue Chicago, IL 60609
Phone Number: (773) 535-1625
Fax Number: (773) 535-1581

Web Site: www.tildenhs.com
E-mail: See Web site
Principal: Ms. Phyllis Hammond
Admissions Contact: Ms. Judith Placzek
Gender: Coed

Total Enrollment: 1,000	*Student to Faculty Ratio:* 20:1
Number of Freshmen: 500	*Percentage of College Bound Grads:* 50%
Average Class Size: 28	*Tuition:* N/A

Other Expenditures: N/A
Academic Specialty: College and career prep
Honors/Advanced Placement Classes: Yes
International Baccalaureate Program: No
Resources, Special Learning Needs: Yes
Profile: Est. 1890. Bridgeport. Schools-within-a-school. Freshman Academy eases transition. Education-to-Careers programs. JROTC. Academy of Finance. International Language and Career Academy.
Unique Traits: Curriculum based on Small Learning Concepts (SLC) model
Public Transportation:
    CTA Bus: Halsted
Dress Code: Black slacks or skirt, white shirt with collar
Admission Requirements: Priority given to students living in attendance area
Academic Scholarships: N/A

Jacqueline Vaughn Occupational High School

4355 North Linder Avenue Chicago, IL 60641
Phone Number: (773) 534-3600
Fax Number: (773) 534-3631

Web Site: www.vaughn.cps.k12.il.us
E-mail: See Web site
Principal: Ms. Nancy J. Mayer
Admissions Contact: Ms. Catalina Fernandez
Gender: Coed

Total Enrollment: 230	*Student to Faculty Ratio:* 15:1
Number of Freshmen: 45	*Percentage of College Bound Grads:* N/A
Average Class Size: 15	*Tuition:* N/A

Other Expenditures: N/A
Academic Specialty: Career prep
Honors/Advanced Placement Classes: No
International Baccalaureate Program: No
Resources, Special Learning Needs: Yes
Profile: Est.1993. Portage Park. Special education facility for students
with mild to moderate cognitive disabilities. Occupational programs
available in business, hospitality, and service. Individual program of
instruction. Focus on social and emotional growth.
Unique Traits: A 100% special education high school
Public Transportation:
    CTA L: Blue Line Jefferson Park
    CTA Bus: Montrose
Dress Code: Appropriate casual; jeans acceptable
Admission Requirements: Accepts students assessed with disabilities liv-
ing north of Roosevelt Road (1200 South)
Academic Scholarships: N/A

Moses Vine Preparatory Academy

730 North Pulaski Road Chicago, IL 60624
Phone Number: (773) 534-8808
Fax Number: (773) 534-8945

Web Site: www.vines.cps.k12.il.us
E-mail: See Web site
Principal: Ms. Patricia Woodson, Interim Principal
Admissions Contact: Ms. Jacqueline Robinson
Gender: Coed

Total Enrollment: 375   *Student to Faculty Ratio:* 25:1
Number of Freshmen: 160   *Percentage of College Bound Grads:* 20%
Average Class Size: 25   *Tuition:* N/A

Other Expenditures: N/A
Academic Specialty: College prep
Honors/Advanced Placement Classes: Yes
International Baccalaureate Program: No
Resources, Special Learning Needs: Yes
Profile: 2002. West side. Small school located in the former Orr High
    School. Programs for every level of learning skills. Family and local
    community support. Classes taught in the Paideia model.
Unique Traits: Freshman Mastery program builds reading and math
    skills
Public Transportation:
    CTA L: Green Line Pulaski
    CTA Bus: Pulaski, Chicago
Dress Code: Any solid color slacks or skirt, school polo shirt
Admission Requirements: Priority given to students living in attendance
    area
Academic Scholarships: N/A

Frederick Von Steuben
Metropolitan Science Center

5039 North Kimball Avenue Chicago, IL 60625
Phone Number: (773) 534-5100
Fax Number: (773) 534-5210

Web Site: www.vonsteuben.org
E-mail: See Web site
Principal: Mr. Clifton D. Burgess
Admissions Contact: Ms. Annette Gonzalez
Gender: Coed

Total Enrollment: 1,500   *Student to Faculty Ratio:* 24:1
Number of Freshmen: 450   *Percentage of College Bound Grads:* 80%
Average Class Size: 28   *Tuition:* N/A

Other Expenditures: N/A
Academic Specialty: College prep
Honors/Advanced Placement Classes: Yes
International Baccalaureate Program: No
Resources, Special Learning Needs: Yes
Profile: Est. 1934. Albany Park. Magnet school. Rigorous academic program specializing in technology and science. Education-to-Careers programs. Scholars program listed in *U.S. News & World Report*'s "96 Outstanding American High Schools," January 1999 and *Newsweek*'s "100 Top Public High Schools," 2003 and 2005.
Unique Traits: One of three Illinois high schools with membership to the National Consortium of Specialized Secondary Schools
Public Transportation:
     CTA L: Brown Line Kimball
Dress Code: Appropriate casual; jeans acceptable
Admission Requirements: Accepts freshmen students citywide; random lottery
Academic Scholarships: N/A

William H. Wells Community Academy High School

936 North Ashland Avenue Chicago, IL 60622
Phone Number: (773) 534-7010
Fax Number: (773) 534-7078

Web Site: www.wells.cps.k12.il.us
E-mail: See Web site
Principal: Mr. Oswaldo Alfaro
Admissions Contact: Ms. Alma Delgado
Gender: Coed

Total Enrollment: 1,100   *Student to Faculty Ratio:* 15:1
Number of Freshmen: 300   *Percentage of College Bound Grads:* 60%
Average Class Size: 28   *Tuition:* N/A

Other Expenditures: N/A
Academic Specialty: College and career prep
Honors/Advanced Placement Classes: Yes
International Baccalaureate Program: No
Resources, Special Learning Needs: Yes
Profile: Est. 1935. West Town. Law and Public Safety Academy. Education-to-Careers programs. Technology Academy.
Unique Traits: Program variety
Public Transportation:
    CTA Bus: Ashland
Dress Code: Black slacks or skirt, white shirt with collar. Appropriate casual; jeans acceptable
Admission Requirements: Priority given to students living in attendance area
Academic Scholarships: N/A

Whitney Young Magnet High School

211 South Laflin Street Chicago, IL 60607
Phone Number: (773) 534-7500
Fax Number: (773) 534-7261

Web Site: www.wyoung.org
E-mail: See Web site
Principal: Dr. Joyce Kenner
Admissions Contact: Ms. Lynn Zalon
Gender: Coed

Total Enrollment: 2,170
Number of Freshmen: 450
Average Class Size: 28

Student to Faculty Ratio: 20:1
Percentage of College Bound Grads: 100%
Tuition: N/A

Other Expenditures: N/A
Academic Specialty: College prep
Honors/Advanced Placement Classes: Yes
International Baccalaureate Program: No
Resources, Special Learning Needs: Yes
Profile: Est. 1975. West Loop. Selective Enrollment School. Rigorous curriculum. One of the largest Advanced Placement (AP) programs in the city. JROTC. Listed in *U.S. News & World Report*'s "96 Outstanding American High Schools," January 1999.
Unique Traits: In 2004 had 24 National Achievement semifinalists, the highest number in the nation
Public Transportation:
   CTA L: Blue Line Racine
   CTA Bus: Jackson, Madison
Dress Code: Appropriate casual; jeans acceptable
Admission Requirements: Accepts students citywide; entrance exam, transcripts
Academic Scholarships: N/A

Youth Connection Charter School

10 West 35th Street Chicago, IL 60616
Phone Number: (312) 328-0799
Fax Number: (312) 328-0971

Web Site: www.yccs.org
E-mail: See web site
Principal: Ms. Sheila Venson, Director
Admissions Contact: Ms. Doris Whittman
Gender: Coed

Total Enrollment: 2,200	*Student to Faculty Ratio:* 20:1
Number of Freshmen: N/A	*Percentage of College Bound Grads:* 50%
Average Class Size: 12–20	*Tuition:* N/A

Other Expenditures: N/A
Academic Specialty: Career prep
Honors/Advanced Placement Classes: N/A
International Baccalaureate Program: N/A
Resources, Special Learning Needs: N/A
Profile: Est. 1997. Charter school headquarters. Small schools. 23 campuses throughout the city. Caters to students that have dropped out of high school. Focuses on life skills, self-esteem, and job placement. High success rate.
Unique Traits: The largest public education entity in the city of Chicago
Public Transportation: Varies by campus
Dress Code: Varies by campus
Admission Requirements: Must be between 16 and 20 years old. Contact headquarters for information on individual schools
Academic Scholarships: N/A

Making the Call

A Public Coed High School Experience

By K.B.

After everything my daughter had been through (she had been ill during her seventh grade year) it was very important to me that she attend the high school of her choice. Most of her friends had applied to all-girls Catholic schools as well as other private schools in the city, but she announced that she wanted to attend a large, public high school. She was looking forward to the diversity and excited by the sheer size of the school. It was the adventure she deserved, and I supported her decision wholeheartedly.

I cannot honestly say that my daughter's Catholic grammar school shared in our enthusiasm. They felt very strongly that it was not the place for her. Since I couldn't count on their support, I had to go it alone. But, where to start?

The first edition of this book provided me with accurate information so I could stop listening to other parents as they shared each other's hearsay. Now that I knew what programs were available and what the admission requirements were, I felt less intimidated. I decided to take a chance, call the admissions director of her first-choice school, and discuss my daughter's special situation. The director's name was listed in the book and, believe me, it makes a big difference to know whom to ask for when you call.

The director was impressed with the fact that my daughter had been able to get the grades she had, considering the circumstances. Not only did the director send me an application, she signed her name on it to assure it would be brought to her attention when we sent it back, and requested I include a note reminding her of our discussion. My daughter was accepted, and we were given the good news earlier than expected. As her apprehensive classmates and their stressed parents awaited their acceptance letters, I was grateful that, for us, the process was over.

The entire process was easy compared to my experience helping my son research high schools the year before. I remember countless open houses, high school nights, and mounds of paper to go through. In contrast, and largely due to the help this book gave me, this time, the whole process was streamlined.

A large, public school may not be the right spot for everyone, but my daughter was ready for a change, and, honestly, now that I see how she's developed, I think this may have been more her style all along. My daughter has flourished in her new environment. As a parent, I couldn't ask for more than that.

Young Women's Leadership Charter School

2641 South Calumet Street Chicago, IL 60616
Phone Number: (312) 949-9400
Fax Number: (312) 949-9142

Web Site: www.ywlcs.org
E-mail: See Web site
Principal: Ms. Mary Ann Pitcher and Ms. Margaret Small, Codirectors
Admissions Contact: Ms. Felicia Ellington
Gender: Girls

Total Enrollment: 325	*Student to Faculty Ratio:* 15:1
Number of Freshmen: 75	*Percentage of College Bound Grads:* 95%
Average Class Size: 25	*Tuition:* N/A

Other Expenditures: N/A
Academic Specialty: College prep
Honors/Advanced Placement Classes: Yes
International Baccalaureate Program: No
Resources, Special Learning Needs: Yes
Profile: Est. 2000. Bronzeville. Small school. Rigorous curriculum for low-income female minority students. Modeled after East Harlem, New York school. Focus on math, science, technology, and leadership. One-on-one mentoring by professional women for four years.
Unique Traits: The only all-girl public school in Chicago and the only charter school of its kind
Public Transportation:
    CTA Bus: State
Dress Code: Appropriate casual; jeans acceptable
Admission Requirements: Accepts students citywide; random lottery
Academic Scholarships: N/A

Other High School Options

Introduction

These are schools that are neither Catholic, independent, nor public and have no group affiliation. Whether they are religion based, nontraditional, or one of a kind, they are gaining recognition for their unique qualities.

When reviewing other high school options, look for special designations and awards given to schools. *U.S. News & World Report* and the *Wall Street Journal* did include some of these high schools in their reports of outstanding high schools.

Since every school offers financial aid, no separate heading for it appears in the individual school listings. There are literally millions of dollars made available each year to those students who qualify.

High school fairs offer a way to obtain an overview of many schools, which may entice you to plan a visit or to give a school a second look. For timely information on high school fairs, contact the individual school.

Other High School Options: Coed

Chicago Hope Academy

2189 West Bowler Street Chicago, IL 60612
Phone Number: (312) 491-1600
Fax Number: (312) 491-1616

Web Site: www.chicagohopeacademy.com
E-mail: information@chicagohopeacademy.com
Principal: Mr. Brad Perry, Dean of Students
Admissions Contact: Ms. Cassie King, Ms. Lindrey Anderson
Gender: Coed

Total Enrollment: 66	*Student to Faculty Ratio:* 6:1
Number of Freshmen: 48	*Percentage of College Bound Grads:* N/A
Average Class Size: 12–16	*Tuition:* $$

Other Expenditures: Yes, also field trips
Academic Specialty: College prep
Honors/Advanced Placement Classes: Yes
International Baccalaureate Program: No
Resources, Special Learning Needs: No
Profile: Est. 2005. Near west side. Private Christian school dedicated to nurturing and challenging the whole person: body, mind, and spirit. Christ-centered education; the Bible is a core subject.
Unique Traits: Work-study programs, after-school study hall, small classes
Public Transportation:
>   CTA L: Blue Line Western, University Medical Center
>   CTA Bus: Taylor, Ogden
Dress Code: Navy slacks or skirt, white shirt, tie for boys
Admission Requirements: Application, placement exam, recommendations, family interview
Academic Scholarships: Yes

Illinois Mathematics and Science Academy

1500 West Sullivan Road Aurora, IL 60506
Phone Number: (630) 907-5028
Fax Number: (630) 907-5887

Web Site: www.imsa.edu
E-mail: aconyers@imsa.edu
Principal: Mr. Eric McLaren
Admissions Contact: Ms. Amy Conyers
Gender: Coed

Total Enrollment: 650	*Student to Faculty Ratio:* 10:1
Number of Freshmen: 230	*Percentage of College Bound Grads:* 99%
Average Class Size: 18–24	*Tuition:* State funded; no tuition, room/board

Other Expenditures: Activities fee based on family income; sliding scale of $250–$2,000 per year

Academic Specialty: College prep

Honors/Advanced Placement Classes: Yes

International Baccalaureate Program: No

Resources, Special Learning Needs: No

Profile: Est. 1986. Grades 10–12. Illinois' only 3 year residential college prep program. First-class curriculum. Individual research opportunities. Nobel prize–winning physicist as resident scholar. Integrated curriculum. Mentorship program. Ranked "One of the Top Ten Public Schools in the Nation" by the *Wall Street Journal.*

Unique Traits: The only school of its kind

Public Transportation:

      Pace Bus: Sullivan

      Metra: Aurora

Dress Code: Appropriate casual; jeans acceptable

Admission Requirements: Application; principal, counselor, and teacher (math, science, English) recommendations; SAT I score report; transcripts

Academic Scholarships: No

Luther High School North

5700 West Berteau Avenue Chicago, IL 60634
Phone Number: (773) 286-3600
Fax Number: (773) 286-0304

Web Site: www.luthernorth.org
E-mail: rschaefer@luthernorth.org
Principal: Dr. Jeff Daley
Admissions Contact: Mr. Ron Schaefer
Gender: Coed

Total Enrollment: 260	*Student to Faculty Ratio:* 22:1
Number of Freshmen: 75	*Percentage of College Bound Grads:* 85%
Average Class Size: 22	*Tuition:* $$

Other Expenditures: Yes
Academic Specialty: College prep
Honors/Advanced Placement Classes: Yes
International Baccalaureate Program: No
Resources, Special Learning Needs: Yes, limited
Profile: Est. 1953. Portage Park. Campus is one city block, located in a residential community. Sports programs utilize Portage Park (one of the city's largest). Dedicated to the Lutheran tradition; to serve God by developing productive and responsible Christian servant-leaders for church and society.
Unique Traits: Embarking on a Special Services program, taught by a fully certified special education teacher
Public Transportation:
> CTA L: Blue Line Montrose, Jefferson Park, Irving Park
> CTA Bus: Irving Park, Central, Montrose
Dress Code: Appropriate casual; jeans acceptable
Admission Requirements: Placement exam, transcripts
Academic Scholarships: Yes

Luther High School South

3130 West 87th Street Chicago, IL 60652
Phone Number: (773) 737-1416
Fax Number: (773) 737-2882

Web Site: www.luthersouth.org
E-mail: See Web site
Principal: Mr. Anthony Rainey
Admissions Contact: Ms. Chassie Davis
Gender: Coed

Total Enrollment: 260   *Student to Faculty Ratio:* 14:1
Number of Freshmen: 74   *Percentage of College Bound Grads:* 99%
Average Class Size: 15–25   *Tuition:* $$

Other Expenditures: Yes
Academic Specialty: College prep
Honors/Advanced Placement Classes: Yes
International Baccalaureate Program: No
Resources, Special Learning Needs: Yes, limited
Profile: Est. 1951. Evergreen Park. 22-acre campus. Student population is
   98% African American. Established in the Lutheran tradition; ethi-
   cal and moral values. Winner of the Christus Award for education in
   Lutheran secondary schools.
Unique Traits: The only predominately African American Lutheran high
   school in the nation
Public Transportation:
   CTA Bus: 87th
Dress Code: Appropriate casual; jeans acceptable
Admission Requirements: Placement exam, transcripts
Academic Scholarships: Based on entrance exam

Timothy Christian High School

1061 South Prospect Avenue Elmhurst, IL 60126
Phone Number: (630) 833-7575
Fax Number: (630) 833-9821

Web Site: www.timothychristian.com
E-mail: raley@timothychristian.com
Principal: Mr. Clyde Rinsema
Admissions Contact: Ms. Ann Raley
Gender: Coed

Total Enrollment: 397	*Student to Faculty Ratio:* Not available
Number of Freshmen: 90	*Percentage of College Bound Grads:* 97%
Average Class Size: Varies	*Tuition:* $$

Other Expenditures: Yes, also family building/maintenance fee, student activity fee

Academic Specialty: College prep

Honors/Advanced Placement Classes: Yes

International Baccalaureate Program: No

Resources, Special Learning Needs: Yes

Profile: Est. 1911. Grades Pre-K–12. Teaches from a reformed Christian perspective. Listed in *U.S. News & World Report*'s "96 Outstanding American High Schools," January 1999.

Unique Traits: Curriculum reflects the reformed Christian worldview

Public Transportation: Bus transportation included in tuition (contact school for more information)

Dress Code: Appropriate casual; jeans acceptable

Admission Requirements: One parent must be an active member of a Christian Church (verified by their clergy), application, transcripts

Academic Scholarships: N/A

Resource Guide

Academic Enrichment and Scholarship Resources

Tutoring, mentoring, and scholarshp opportunities for low-income students.

A Better Chance
(646) 346-1310
www.abetterchance.org

Big Shoulders Fund
(312) 751-8337
www.bigshouldersfund.org

Daniel Murphy Scholarship Fund
(312) 455-7808
www.dmsf.org

High Jump
(312) 582-7700
www.highjumpchicago.org

HighSight
(312) 787-9824
www.highsight.org

Link Unlimited
(773) 487-5465
www.linkunlimited.org

PEAK (Partnership to Educate and Advance Kids)
(773) 975-6540
www.peakchicago.org

General Resources

Blue Ribbon Schools
Information about the program and listings of schools
www.ed.gov (search: blue ribbon schools)

Chicago Transit Authority (CTA)
Schedules, fares, maps, trip planner
(888) 968-7282
www.transitchicago.com

Gender-Specific Learning Styles
Research presenting the pros and cons of single-sex education
www.eric.ed.gov (search: single sex schools)

Catholic High Schools Resources

Archdiocese profile, school search, school profiles
(312) 751-5200
www.archdiocese-chgo.org/schools

Independent High Schools Resources

Lake Michigan Association of Independent Schools
Chicago area member schools, map, application process
www.independentschools.net

National Association of Independent Schools
Background information, school search, admissions, financial aid
(202) 973-9700
www.nais.org

Entrance Exams
For information: Educational Records Bureau
(800) 989-3721
To register: www.iseetest.org

Public High Schools Resources

Core strategies, school directory, student and parent
    information
Office of High School Programs: (773) 553-3540
www.cps.k12.il.us

Glossary of Public High School Special Programs

Academy of Finance
This nationally approved, four-year college preparatory program offers mentoring, workplace experience, and finance-related courses in financial planning, banking, insurance, international finance, and accounting in addition to an academic curriculum. Students may earn tuition-free college credit hours and obtain a paid internship.

Career Academy
Some Chicago public schools have been designated a Career Academy. They offer a college prep curriculum combined with a career-focused education in various fields. Students visit local businesses and may also shadow with business professionals.

CISCO Program
This program trains students to design, install, and maintain computer networks and prepares them to take industry certification exams through hands-on training, work experience, and classroom instruction.

Colloquium Program
Inspired by the Greek philosopher Socrates these academic programs allow small groups of students to examine a single subject in detail.

Education-to-Careers Program

This program combines academics with work experience to prepare the student for employment, training, or college.

Fine and Performing Arts Program

Enhanced by interaction with Chicago area artists and art institutions, this program allows students to combine an academic curriculum with the study of art, music, dance, or drama.

International Language and Career Academy

This program combines fluency in a foreign language with skills in such fields as international business, hospitality, travel/tourism, culinary arts, and engineering.

Junior Reserve Officers Training Corps (JROTC)

In addition to their high school curriculum, students receive military training within a specific branch of the military in this unique, four-year program.

Law and Public Safety Academy

This program prepares students for a career in law, criminal justice, and corporate security by combining academic and vocational instruction with field experience.

Mathematics, Science, and Technology Academy

This rigorous program offers state-of-the-art science and technology labs as well as AP courses.

Medical Career Academy

A state-of-the-art program that includes corporate-sponsored workplace experience, summer enrichment, and advanced academics. It prepares students for careers in healthcare fields such as medicine, pharmacy, nursing, health systems management, optometry, and dentistry.

Metropolitan Studies

This program incorporates the cultural aspects of Chicago into all areas of its curriculum and expands a student's opportunity with regard to urban resources.

Paideia Program

This demanding science and liberal arts program is based on the Socratic seminar, which develops cognitive skills.

Scholar's Program

This academic program offers challenging honors and AP courses. Students must qualify to receive dual high school and college credits.

Technology Academy

This program prepares students for occupations in computer operation, programming, information processing, repair, and installation. Designed as a school-within-a-school, the program allows eligible students to earn industry certification upon graduation.

World Language and International Studies Program

This college prep program for gifted students emphasizes fluency in a foreign language, development of international communication skills, and the study of global issues.

Alphabetical Index

Index by Tuition Category

$: Less than $6,000

Catholic Boys
Hales Franciscan High School, 7
Leo High School, 8

Catholic Girls
Josephinum Academy, 16
Mount Assisi Academy, 19
Our Lady of Tepeyac High School, 21

Catholic Coed
Cristo Rey Jesuit High School, 28

$$: $6,000–$8,000

Catholic Boys
Archbishop Quigley Preparatory Seminary High School, 5
Brother Rice High School, 6
Mount Carmel High School, 9
Notre Dame High School, 10
St. Lawrence Seminary High School, 11
St. Patrick High School, 12
St. Rita of Cascia High School, 13

Catholic Girls
Maria High School, 17
Mother McAuley Liberal Arts High School, 18
Notre Dame High School, 20
Queen of Peace High School, 22
Resurrection High School, 24
St. Scholastica Academy, 25
Trinity High School, 26

Catholic Coed
De La Salle Institute, 29
Gordon Tech High School, 31
Guerin College Preparatory High School, 32
Holy Trinity High School, 33
Marist High School, 35
St. Benedict High School, 37
St. Francis de Sales High School, 38
St. Gregory High School, 39
St. Joseph High School, 41
Seton Academy, 43

Other High School Options Coed
Chicago Hope Academy, 169
Luther High School North, 171
Luther High School South, 172
Timothy Christian High Schoo, 173

$$$: $8,000–$10,000

Catholic Girls
Regina Dominican High School, 23

Catholic Coed
Fenwick High School, 30
Loyola Academy, 34
Nazareth Academy, 36
St. Ignatius College Prep High School, 40
St. Viator High School, 42

Independent Boys
Northridge Prep School, 50

Independent Girls
Willows Academy, 52

$$$$: $10,000–$15,000

Independent Coed
Chicago Academy for the Arts, 54
Chicago Waldorf School, 55
Morgan Park Academy, 60

$$$$$: Over $15,000

Catholic Girls
Woodlands Academy of the Sacred Heart, 27

Independent Boys
St. John's Northwestern Military Academy, 51

Independent Coed
British School of Chicago, 53
Howe Military School, 56
Lake Forest Academy, 57
La Lumiere School, 58

Index by Zip Code

60093

North Shore Country Day School (independent, coed), 61

60126

Timothy Christian High School (other option, coed), 173

60154

St. Joseph High School (Catholic, coed), 41

60171

Guerin College Preparatory High School (Catholic, coed), 32

60201

Roycemore School (independent, ceod), 63

60302

Fenwick High School (Catholic, coed), 30

60305

Trinity High School (Catholic, girls), 26

60439

Mount Assisi Academy (Catholic, girls), 19

60459

Queen of Peace High School (Catholic, girls), 22

60473

Seton Academy (Catholic, coed), 43

60506

Illinois Mathematics and Science Academy (other option, coed), 170

60526

Nazareth Academy (Catholic, coed), 36

60605

Jones College Preparatory High School (public, coed), 114

60607

Whitney M. Young Magnet High School (public, coed), 161

60608

Benito Juarez Community Academy (public, coed), 115
Cristo Rey Jesuit High School (Catholic, coed), 28
St. Ignatius College Prep High School (Catholic, coed), 40

60609

Architecture, Construction and Engineering (ACE) Technical
    High School (public, coed), 75
Big Picture Company High School at Back of the Yards (public,
    coed), 77
Ellen H. Richards Career Academy High School (public, coed),
    142
Edward Tilden Career Community Academy (public, coed), 156
Las Casas Occupational High School (public, coed), 124

60610

Latin School of Chicago (independent, coed), 59
Walter Payton College Preparatory High School (public, coed),
    136

60611

Archbishop Quigley Preparatory Seminary High School (Catho-
    lic, boys), 5

60612

Chicago Hope Academy (other option, coed), 169

Richard T. Crane Technical Preparatory Common School (public, coed), 95

Hugh Manley Career Academy High School (public, coed), 127

Phoenix Military Academy (public, coed), 138

60613

Lake View High School (public, coed), 122

60614

Lincoln Park High School (public, coed), 125

Francis W. Parker School (independent, coed), 62

60615

DuSable Multiplex Campus (public, coed), 98

Walter H. Dyett Academic Center (public, coed), 99

Hales Franciscan High School (Catholic, boys), 7

Kenwood Academy (public, coed), 120

60616

De La Salle Institute (Catholic, coed), 29

Paul L. Dunbar Vocational Career Academy (public, coed), 97

Young Women's Leadership Charter School (public, girls), 165

Youth Connection Charter School (public, coed), 162

60617

Bowen Environmental Studies Team (BEST) High School (public, coed), 79

Chicago Discovery Academy (public, coed), 83

Global Visions Academy (public, coed), 106

New Millennium School of Health (public, coed), 131

St. Francis de Sales High School (Catholic, coed), 38

60618

Gordon Tech High School (Catholic, coed), 31
Lane Tech College Prep High School (public, coed), 123
St. Benedict High School (Catholic, coed), 37

60619

Hirsch Metropolitan High School of Communications (public, coed), 110

60620

Big Picture Company High School at Williams (public, coed), 77
Leo High School (Catholic, boys), 8
Neal F. Simeon Career Academy High School (public, coed), 151
St. Rita of Cascia High School (Catholic, boys), 13

60621

Englewood Technical Preparatory Academy (public, coed), 100
John Hope College Preparatory High School (public, coed), 111
Paul Robeson High School (public, coed), 143

60622

Chicago Academy for the Arts (independent, coed), 54
Roberto Clemente Community Academy High School (public, coed), 91
Holy Trinity High School (Catholic, coed), 33
Josephinum Academy (Catholic, girls), 16
Noble Street Charter High School (public, coed), 132
William H. Wells Community Academy High School (public, coed), 160

60623

George Washington Collins High School (public, coed), 92
Community Links High School (public, coed), 93

David Glasgow Farragut Career Academy (public, coed), 102
North Lawndale College Preparatory Charter High School
(public, coed), 134
Our Lady of Tepeyac High School (Catholic, girls), 21

60624

Academy of Applied Arts, Science and Technology High School
(public, coed), 72
Academy of Communications and Technology Charter High
School (public, coed), 73
Excel Academy (public, coed), 101
John Marshall Metropolitan High School (public, coed), 128
Al Raby High School for Community and Environment (public,
coed), 140
Moses Vine Preparatory Academy (public, coed), 158

60625

Amundsen High School (public, coed), 74
Northside College Preparatory High School (public, coed), 135
Theodore Roosevelt High School (public, coed), 144
Frederick Von Steuben Metropolitan Science Center (public,
coed), 159

60626

Chicago Mathematics and Science Academy Charter School
(public, coed), 87
Chicago Waldorf School (independent, coed), 55
Roger C. Sullivan High School (public, coed), 154

60628

Gwendolyn Brooks College Preparatory Academy (public, coed),
80
George H. Corliss High School (public, coed), 94

Christian Fenger Academy High School (public, coed), 103
John Marshall Harlan Community Academy (public, coed), 108

60629
Gage Park High School (public, coed), 105
John Hancock High School (public, coed), 107
Gordon S. Hubbard High School (public, coed), 112
Maria High School (Catholic, girls), 117

60631
Resurrection High School (Catholic, girls), 24
William Howard Taft High School (public, coed), 155

60632
Curie Metropolitan High School (public, coed), 96
Thomas Kelly High School (public, coed), 117

60634
Chicago Academy High School (public, coed), 82
Luther High School North (other option, coed), 171
Notre Dame High School (Catholic, girls), 20
St. Patrick High School (Catholic, boys), 12
Charles P. Steinmetz Academic Centre (public, coed), 153

60636
William Rainey Harper High School (public, coed), 109
Southside Occupational Academy (public, coed), 152

60637
Hyde Park Academy (public, coed), 113
Mount Carmel High School (Catholic, boys), 9
University of Chicago Laboratory School (independent, coed),
    64

60638

John F. Kennedy High School (public, coed), 119

60639

Kelvyn Park High School (public, coed), 118

North Grand High School (public, coed), 133

Charles A. Prosser Career Academy (public, coed), 139

60641

Edwin G. Foreman High School (public, coed), 104

Carl Schurz High School (public, coed), 149

Jacqueline Vaughn Occupational High School (public, coed), 157

60643

Chicago International Charter School—Longwood (public, coed), 85

Percy L. Julian High School (public, coed), 116

Morgan Park Academy (independent, coed), 60

Morgan Park High School (public, coed), 130

60644

Michele Clark Academic Preparatory High School (public, coed), 90

Robert Lindblom College Preparatory High School (public, coed), 126

60645

St. Scholastica Academy (Catholic, girls), 25

60647

Mirta Ramirez Computer Science Charter School (public, coed), 141

60649

School of the Arts High School (public, coed), 145
School of Entrepreneurship High School (public, coed), 146
School of Leadership High School (public, coed), 147
School of Technology High School (public, coed), 148

60652

William J. Bogan Computer Technical High School (public, coed), 78
Luther High School South (other option, coed), 172

60653

Chicago Military Academy—Bronzeville (public, coed), 88
Dr. Martin Luther King Jr. College Preparatory High School (public, coed), 121
Wendell Phillips Academy High School (public, coed), 137

60655

Brother Rice High School (Catholic, boys), 6
Chicago High School for Agricultural Sciences (public, coed), 84
Marist High School (Catholic, coed), 35
Mother McAuley Liberal Arts High School (Catholic, girls), 18

60659

Chicago International Charter High School—Northtown Academy (public, coed), 86
Stephen Tyng Mather High School (public, coed), 129

60660

British School of Chicago (independent, coed), 53
Nicholas Senn High School (public, coed), 150
St. Gregory High School (Catholic, coed), 39

60714
Northridge Prep School (independent, boys), 50
Notre Dame High School (Catholic,boys), 10

60827
George Washington Carver Military Academy (public, coed), 81

66017
Chicago Vocational Career Academy (public, coed), 89